BUTTS IN SEATS

HOW TO CREATE RAVING FANS
WHO COME BACK AGAIN AND AGAIN

GREG PROVANCE

Melissa,

Thank you for your amazing example of leadership...

So wonderful to be a part of the Pinnacle Family!

love
Greg

For more information or for book orders, address:
greg@GPHospitalityPartners.com

First paperback edition March 2021

Book editing by Phoenix Bunke

Book design by Laeeq Hussain Arif

ISBN 978-1-5136-8064-4

Library of Congress Control Number: 2021900991

www.GPHospitalityPartners.com

Contents

INTRODUCTION

"If anything is good for pounding humility into you permanently, it's the restaurant business." – Anthony Bourdain

When I was almost fifteen years old, I got hired at my first job at Popeye's Chicken. They paid me minimum wage, which at the time was a whopping $3.35 per hour. Over the summer months, the busiest time of the year for a restaurant located in the heart of the tourist section of the Virginia Beach oceanfront, I regularly worked thirty to forty hours a week. Soon, I conspired to get several more of my friends hired. We had a blast, frying chicken over sizzling vats, battering and adding the signature spice to each batch, and spending hours scrubbing and cleaning after the shift. It was my greasy, grimy introduction to restaurant life. And I loved it.

After that summer, I went on to work in various areas of hospitality. As a hotel valet and bellman at an oceanfront resort, I first learned the art of getting to know Guests as a way to garner better tips. Admittedly, at that point, hospitality had a purpose for me, which was to make as much money as I could. I began to cultivate the skill of working with a sense of urgency and supporting the needs of an entire team by bussing tables at a busy seafood buffet. My first experience working behind the bar was shucking oysters at a raw bar. After hours, the bartenders would teach me how to make drinks and shooters for them, evenings of camaraderie that built the foundation of my bartending career.

As the years went on, besides one short stint working construction, I worked exclusively in restaurants and bars, cultivating my skills at every single position one could master in the industry. From washing dishes to cooking on the kitchen line to serving and managing—you name it, I've done it. From that humble beginning frying chicken, I went on to own my own businesses, most of them restaurants, all of them centered around the art of food, drinks, service and hospitality.

In all that time, being of service to others is something I have never grown tired of. Indirectly participating in so many people's life events, sometimes as a host and other times simply as a fly on the wall, creates an astonishing array of opportunities for human connection. I have had the great fortune of sharing intimate moments with friends, family, neighbors, and complete strangers. I have hosted parties and worked events for celebrities like Janet Jackson, Madonna, Tom Cruise, Eve, Stevie Wonder and DL Hughley,—to name a select few. I have served food and beverages in atmospheres that range from dive bars to the Oscars, from Suffolk, Virginia, to Beverly Hills, and pretty much everything in between.

And, after everything I have experienced, one simple fact rings true: Regardless of the establishment, the type of food, or who is in attendance, we are simply people serving people. The basis of the hospitality industry is people coming together to help one another experience something, and, depending on the nature of the gathering, in that shared space, the most memorable things can happen.

Over the years, I have learned that in the restaurant industry, we have a unique opportunity to become very close to our Guests. We share moments with our fellow human beings on a regular basis. Sometimes, those moments can be quite intimate. People come to our restaurants, bars, cafés and event spaces to live out small pieces of their life stories. Some of those events may be as simple as grabbing a quick coffee on the way to a meeting. Others are as elaborate and life-changing as a dream wedding.

People meet in our spaces to discuss business ventures and make deals. They join close friends for lunch and share memories of old times. They entertain family, friends and business associates in any manner of ways. They honor milestones both triumphant and sorrowful: birthdays, passings, unions and divorces. Some mourn losses and sit sadly at the bar, while some join friends to jubilantly express the joy of coming together. Life happens everywhere, but there are few other arenas in which so many monumental occasions are celebrated with such frequency.

Not only is this circumstance a truly unique and wonderful opportunity for our industry, but it is also an incredible responsibility. Once someone walks through the threshold into the four walls of our business, we take their lives into our hands. It is now our responsibility to discover how, today, at this moment, we can positively influence the experience of each and every one of our Guests. Whatever degree to which we take this responsibility seriously and execute it consistently, that effort shall determine our results. Our success as business owners and managers is directly proportional to how many people we serve and how well we serve them.

The concepts in the pages that follow are not new. I doubt anything in this book will shock and awe those of us who have been doing business for some time. Surely many of us have heard about these ideas and even discussed them with our teams. I would hope you are already implementing many of these strategies and suggestions. However, I can guarantee that only a few of us are consistently able to execute these principles at the level of excellence that we would prefer.

Perhaps that is the reason you bought this book. Perhaps you, like others in our industry, are looking for solutions to a problem we have all faced.

How can we get more butts in seats?

Perhaps you have a business outside of the restaurant and hospitality industry and would like to apply some of these concepts in your own field. There is much that can be learned by stepping outside of your specific area of expertise and applying the knowledge gained from years of serving others to your business.

What this book is not: It's not a crash course in how to get more likes on Facebook or master the art of social media marketing. There are many wonderful books and courses out there that can help you with that. *Butts in Seats* is an organic, grassroots approach to marketing and business growth using all the resources that already reside within the four walls of your business. It aims to give you the knowledge and understanding you need to develop systems and make connections with people within your business, and in so doing, leverage the most powerful marketing force available to you.

Social media, PR firms, print and radio and TV ads, mailers and other forms of direct marketing can be very effective to promote your business, and these options may be something you should be engaging in. But in my experience, without a rock-solid foundation within the four walls of your business, none of these methods will support long-term, meaningful growth.

The road from point A to point B is not always a straight line. Every business and every business owner has the option of multiple paths, each including various degrees of hardship and plenty of pitfalls, obstacles and hazards. These difficulties are simply inherent to the journey. If we believe that success comes easily, without hard work and diligent effort, then we have likely fallen victim to the millions of Facebook and social media ads promising instant success in exchange for trusting a complete stranger. "Just follow my simple system, and you will be driving a Lamborghini and sitting on a gold-plated toilet seat in just six months."

I have yet to meet anyone who has experienced lasting, long-term success without knowing the pain of failure. Bumps and bruises are all part of the game.

As I speak of bumps and bruises, I must acknowledge something that has recently changed the face of history and business, including where the seats might be located and how many butts will be coming in to fill them. Yes, I'm talking about COVID-19. In a time when businesses are struggling to stay afloat, when millions of restaurants have had to shut their doors, temporarily or, sadly, permanently, is it really worth it to be discussing strategies to attract more customers?

I say yes, and I hope you'll follow my logic. In the wake of the great pandemic, almost every business in existence has felt the impact in some form. The restaurant industry has experienced a wide variety of challenges that can seem insurmountable; but it also holds some significant advantages. Unlike many retailers and other businesses that are not deemed "necessary," restaurants rank particularly high on the "we want to feel normal again" scale.

Perhaps for this reason, many restaurants that have been able to pivot, and those that are lucky enough to possess strong takeout and delivery programs or have significant outdoor dining capabilities—especially those in areas that offer year-round outdoor weather—have experienced a boost in sales, even during this unprecedented time.

The fact is that there will always be a market for selling food. Couple that with a genuine need to congregate with others to share experiences around food and drink, and the restaurant industry's long-term outlook is incredibly bright. There will be great upheaval and there may be many tragic losses, but there will also be, in the future, opportunities to rebuild and rebuild better.

There is no more critical time than now to employ the principles explained in this book. People want more than ever to feel safe, cared for and connected with. The experiences that we offer in our restaurants can not only serve to help our Guests feel some sense of normality, but can provide a much-needed connection to humanity, which has been all but snuffed out for some due to weeks of quarantine and social distancing. If our businesses are to survive, we must be able to harness that connection and center our focus on human emotion and experience.

Even if the seats might now be outdoors or tables spread further from one another, the underlying principles I will be discussing in this book remain relevant. Even as we are practicing the guidelines that are necessary to keep our Guests and Team Members safe, we can still offer a true and meaningful synergistic experience through our hospitality and service of others. We all need this authentic experience of connection now more than ever, and we, as restaurant owners and managers, are uniquely positioned to lead the world in this cause, should we be willing to rise to the occasion.

One thing hasn't changed: We as leaders must still be willing to do whatever it takes—trudging through the trenches with our teams in tow, facing every challenge, navigating every obstacle—to come out victorious. The good news is, there are tools to help make the journey easier. We can choose to walk those miles over rough terrain with bare feet, or we can choose to wear boots made especially for the journey.

The chapters that follow are not a promise that the road to glory will be simple. Rather, they are tools and insights that have proven to create positive results over decades of experience. There is no magic formula; only the degree to which we are willing and able to apply certain principles will determine our results.

Many of us will fail simply because we do not have the knowledge or understanding of certain areas of our businesses necessary to be successful. These pages seek to supply some of that knowledge and understanding so that we as leaders may apply it to our own businesses, but with a shorter learning curve and, perhaps, a lesser impact from those inevitable defeats.

Butts in Seats is based on the understanding that we already have all of the tools we need in order to achieve our professional and financial goals.

Chapter One: The "X" Factor explores the elements and art of hospitality. The examples and stories illustrated in this chapter will teach us how to employ important principles that allow us to use exceptional experiences to create raving fans and turn Guests into ambassadors for our brands.

In *Chapter Two: An Inside Job*, we will learn the importance of seeing success as an inside job. Yes, it is often helpful to engage outside assistance when it comes to specific needs, but in my experience, the majority of owners and managers fail to fully utilize the resources and talent already located within the four walls of their businesses.

Chapter Three: Your Unshakeable Service Model teaches that by learning to focus solely on those we serve, we can create a powerful platform from which to operate our businesses. This chapter will introduce the three critical ingredients of Team Member engagement and outline how to implement them to create a highly effective workforce. This chapter will also outline the three critical ingredients of Guest satisfaction and describe how to create standards that will always deliver impeccable results.

Chapter Four: Living the Mission takes a deep dive into the anatomy, purpose and function of a company's mission statement and shows how this important, often-underutilized tool can become more than just a mantra, but a way of being—one with a massive impact on our organizations.

Chapter Five: A Program of Attraction walks us through how to create more impactful, meaningful and effective promotions. We will go beyond the typical means of promoting and advertising to learn how to truly set our brands apart from our competitors and to offer our Guests something they will want to tell others about and return for again and again.

Chapter Six: A Program of Recovery shows how to leverage the opportunity of failure. When things go wrong—and they will—we must have solid systems for recovery, not only to mend the error, but to turn any bad situation into one that builds loyalty in a way few other opportunities can.

The experience of having built, worked with, and consulted for so many organizations, teams and team leaders—across multiple concepts, business models and markets—gives me the confidence to predict positive outcomes for those who diligently apply the ideas described in these pages. My goal is to help your organization become more profitable, more efficient, and, quite frankly, more enjoyable to run, all while setting your brand apart as an industry leader.

Are you ready to join the top ten percent in your industry—those who understand, implement, and execute with clarity and confidence? Are you willing to do what it takes to transform your business into a scalable, profitable brand? If so, then I am excited to partner with you, and I invite you to read on.

As you do, I encourage you to take a good hard look at how you are currently operating your own business and ask yourself the tough questions about what might need to change to catapult you to exactly where you want to be. If you are committed to the process, then you, like so many that we have helped, can and will reap the benefits of our years of collective experience. See you on the inside!

CHAPTER ONE

THE "X" FACTOR

"I've learned that people will forget what you said, people will forget what you did, but people will never forget how you made them feel." – Maya Angelou

———

Let's face it. Sales cure many ills. We always need more butts in seats, more consistently. No business is immune to this fact. People coming through the door equals sales volume. It's really that simple. But getting to that place can feel complicated and at times overwhelming.

Contrary to popular belief, most restaurants do not fail within their first year. In fact, according to studies by expert hospitality researcher Dr. H.G. Parsa, who has studied why restaurants fail since 1996, only fifty-three percent of restaurants fail within the first three years, with only thirty percent failing in the first year. This may be due to a number of factors beyond simply going bankrupt. Nonetheless, the restaurant industry, like many industries, faces many very real challenges.

While it's true that more and more Americans are investing in eating outside of the home, perhaps due to busier lifestyles and longer working hours, the number of restaurants has increased dramatically to follow suit. There are far more choices out there than there used to be, and restaurant owners are faced with the challenge of differentiation among competitors. How can we set ourselves apart? What can we offer that will be more enticing than the place down the block? All of this competition has helped to create a more discerning, savvier Guest. Expectations are much higher than ever before. People know that they have the choice of where to invest their time, money and life experiences. If we are not on point, we risk losing their business forever.

The cost of doing business continues to rise while consumers are increasingly cost-conscious. Finding ways to retain workers while offering a competitive price is becoming more and more challenging. From the cost of land to employment benefits to cost of goods, everything keeps going up, while Guests are looking for more value than ever before, making competing on price and product alone a failing strategy.

This is part of why I am writing this book. I am here to answer some fundamental questions. If competing on price and quality of product are not enough, then what will be our competitive advantage? How indeed will we convey our unique selling proposition so as to attract more of the market share to our business?

The most obvious answer is what most business owners often suggest when asked this very question. In fact, most anyone, when asked what they value in a business above all else, will likely answer the same. Service. Great customer service is cited as THE defining element that will surely set our businesses apart and keep our Guests returning for more of whatever it is that we offer. Right?

While it is true that great service is absolutely essential, the idea that this alone will definitively set us apart is no longer as viable as it used to be. People have caught on. No longer is it acceptable to give subpar service and expect to achieve lasting results in business. Businesses everywhere have taken up the idea that they must put their customers first, and many have found incredible ways to achieve this. Amazon has revolutionized the art of fast, easy, and accessible products while giving great customer service along the way. Hotels across the globe, such as Hyatt's Andaz brand, go the extra mile to make the Guest experience incredible with innovations like personal check-in services, where, rather than standing at the counter, roaming front desk clerks check Guests in while they sit in the lounge, offering coffee or tea in the process.

I guarantee that our competition, whoever they may be, has already changed their model to accommodate a Guest-first mentality, and they are focusing on service standards constantly. If we are not already doing the same, then we are doomed to be left behind.

In reality, service itself is no longer enough to set us apart. It is expected, a baseline standard, just the same as good quality food, ambiance, and fair prices. People expect great service, and if they do not receive it, they are not likely to return. They will migrate to our competitors because our competitors have already integrated this into their culture and their strategy for success.

If this is true, then what are we left to do? We are back to the same question that brought us to this point. What can and will set us apart from the rest?

The answer lies in what I refer to as "the X factor."

We've all experienced someone who has that certain quality about them that is just magnetic. The person who walks into the room and seems to command its energy just by virtue of who they are. There's just something about the person that others want to be around. It's that "je ne sais quoi," the unexplainable quality that the person possesses.

There are certain businesses that we have all walked into whose atmosphere seems bright and energetically charged. You just walk in and feel good. Conversely, we have all entered spaces that are just dead. These spaces feel like energy vacuums, and even though the sign may say "welcome," we somehow feel that we are not.

There is a small café on the corner in my neighborhood that is like this. This sign outside is inviting, the building is beautiful, the ceilings are high, and the decor is nicely arranged. But when I walk in, I feel like I'm imposing upon the business. The people working the counter barely make eye contact. The TVs are on and music is playing, but it doesn't quite match the space. There is just no life there. It feels uncomfortable to walk in.

At the other end of town, there is another café that is much smaller. It's in a less convenient location and parking is somewhat difficult.

Yet the place is bustling with business. When I walk in I can hear great music playing; the people at the counter are bright, energetic, and seem super happy that I arrived. Within a couple of visits, they knew my name. They constantly make suggestions about what I might want to try next. Before I've even had a chance to order, I've received an entire experience that I want to experience again.

There is an X factor involved here. That X factor is pure hospitality.

The Blind Spot

We all have blind spots. When service and hospitality are referred to as the same thing, we have stumbled into one of these prevalent, industry-wide misconceptions that may not even be apparent at first glance. But what a difference understanding this distinction can make. Learning the true nature of hospitality can be an eye-opening, business-changing proposition.

In reality, service and hospitality are quite distinct. Although there is some overlap in their function, the essence of hospitality is far more evolved from the basics of service. Conflating the two can keep us from realizing our full potential and ensuring our Guests want to return again and again. Yet when service and hospitality are practiced in tandem, what is created is a powerful synergistic energy that is incredibly irresistible. At its heart, this book is about creating, maintaining, and leveraging the genuine, positive energy that true hospitality creates in order to grow our businesses from the inside out.

We as owners and managers must be willing to walk into the light. We must remove the blinders and embrace this energy by inviting the heart of hospitality into our spaces and our culture. This is the first step we must take if we want to create a business that by its very nature compels Guests to return again and again, invite everyone they know, and be delighted to spend their hard-earned money. To do this, we must understand how service and hospitality differ and what each of them offers to help transform our businesses from the inside out.

Technically Speaking

The term "service industry" is often reserved for restaurants and the hospitality sector. This is not surprising, since we who work in these spaces have a unique opportunity to be very close to our Guests. We celebrate occasions of all kinds. We host numerous important, impactful life events, from business deals to weddings, from reunions to celebrations of life and everything in between. We often serve others in very intimate ways and we certainly play this role throughout the entire cycle of our engagement while doing business.

But if we look closely, we can see that no matter what business or sector we are engaged in, it too can be considered a service industry. At the end of the day, whether we are selling products or providing services, we are people serving people. This is why most businesses are ultimately judged almost solely on the quality of their customer service.

Fortunately, every day that we work brings us myriad opportunities to serve our Guests in a way that is so memorable that what we offer becomes irresistible. In later chapters, I will go into more practical detail about what doing this looks like. But first, in order for us to take full advantage of each of these opportunities, we must consider the difference between service and hospitality. We can then consider how they work together to create an experience that goes above and beyond anything our competitors offer.

Let's first consider "service" as a word to describe the technical delivery of goods or services from one person to another. In the restaurant industry, we are tasked with ensuring that our Guests receive exactly what they pay for from the moment they contact us to the moment they leave. When a Guest calls for a reservation, we must ensure that all of the details of that reservation are recorded, including special requests, celebrations, and any communication to confirm those details are properly delivered. Once they arrive, they must be shown to their table in a timely manner and greeted warmly by their server. Water must be sent to the table in clean glasses. The flatware must be polished and neatly arranged. Orders must be taken correctly and food delivered with impeccable timing—fresh, hot and presented beautifully. Every step of service must be coordinated to meet our Guests' highest expectations. Coffee and desserts must be offered, and everything must arrive as expected. The bill must be rung correctly, and ideally the Guests should be invited back.

In a busy restaurant, all of these things must be coordinated and timed perfectly. Success requires a great deal of technical effort and people working together in a highly organized fashion. When everything is executed well, it will likely be described by our Guests as "very good service": all of the elements came together to fulfill expectations and support a great experience. On the other hand, if one or more of these aspects are not executed well, the experience will likely be described as one where "the service was poor." On any given day, most restaurants and hotels do a fairly good job of executing at this level. The ones that do not will quickly earn a reputation that will eventually damage their business. Most anyone can point out the winners and losers in their town quite readily.

Enter the X Factor

Now let's consider the next step up. Hospitality picks up where service leaves off. It is the evolution of service. It is what allows us to take an experience from merely "satisfying expectations" to leaving Guests with a lasting, meaningful memory that will motivate them to return again and again. It is the extra mile, and more, that this book's service model is based upon.

Where service is technical, hospitality is emotional. Where service provides what has now become a baseline expectation, hospitality goes above and beyond. Where service makes a Guest feel like they got what they paid for, hospitality makes a Guest feel like they received more value than they could possibly have paid for—like the most important person in the room.

Let's consider the qualities that make "hospitality" unique and different from what most associate with "service". These qualities will hold the key to finding that spark that will bring Guests back to your establishment again and again.

The Heart of Hospitality #1: Hospitality is personal.

The first thing we must understand is that hospitality transcends the technical and enters the realm of the personal. This is part of what sets it apart from just everyday, ho-hum service.

Someone who truly embodies hospitality has a propensity for connecting deeply with others very quickly. This person has a knack for making someone feel like they are the most important person in the room. This feeling comes from offering warmth and authenticity from the onset. It comes from displaying a level of deep confidence and vulnerability at the same time. A person who practices these qualities can make friends with anyone and everyone.

One definition of the word "personality" is the unique combination of patterns that influence behavior, thought, motivation, and emotion in a human being. It is precisely this influence that creates the difference between simply going through the motions of service and becoming something meaningful to those we are serving. This is why I always encourage my teams to let their personalities shine. When that happens in tandem with great service, a true personal connection can be made, and everyone involved can feel the spirit of hospitality.

The Heart of Hospitality #2: Hospitality is sincere.

I'm sure we can all recall a time where multiple things went wrong at a business we were engaging with. I had a recent experience at a hotel where everything just seemed to go wrong. We were ushered to a dirty room, the key to the door only worked half of the time, we could not get service poolside even though we had paid extra for a cabana, and so on. I finally brought my complaints to the desk manager, who listened to what I had to say, but I felt that he was receiving my concerns halfheartedly at best. Though he apologized, he also gave me a lot of excuses, and moreover, I felt zero compassion from him for what I was experiencing. His responses sounded like he knew what to say, but the emotions behind them didn't feel authentic. I have never returned to that property since and probably never will.

People tend to resonate with authenticity. In fact, most can sense when we are not being genuine, and that will be a huge turn-off. It will repel those that we otherwise could have brought into our fold and created fruitful relationships with. In business, the more people we can connect with at this level, the more people we will be able to truly serve, and the more success we will enjoy was a result.

Coming from a place of sincerity requires a willingness to connect with others rather than putting up a fence or defending a position. It requires us to become vulnerable, which can be difficult, especially in a service position. However, this vulnerability is essential. By being sincere in our efforts and in our communication, and by allowing those we are serving to see us as fellow humans trying to connect with them, we send a message that we truly care about their experience. And, as we will continue to explore in more depth later, that intangible feeling always translates eventually into tangible results.

The Heart of Hospitality #3: Hospitality is emotional.

I'd like to take this moment to mention that, unlike many have been led to believe, emotion is a key factor in building business. We will go into this idea in more detail throughout the rest of the book. Here, what matters is to remember that a very important part of the spirit of true hospitality is an excitement to connect with the types of emotions that drive our Guests to want to come back to our establishment again and again and tell their friends to do the same.

The X factor is all about creating emotions that people will never forget. Working within an emotional space, we can provoke visceral reactions in our Guests that last far beyond the moment. Whether negative or positive, visceral emotional responses are a driving force; the combination of cuisine and emotion that we are working with in the restaurant industry can be especially powerful.

Once, when I was a child, my preschool teacher wanted me to eat my peanut butter and jelly sandwich. The smell and taste of the sandwich was unsettling to me, yet the teacher told me that if I did not eat it, my mother was going to be mad. To a small child, this had an incredibly powerful effect, so I ate the sandwich—and quickly threw it back up. To this day, I am repulsed by peanut butter and jelly sandwiches. I love peanut butter. I like jelly. But together, they bring up such a negative emotion that I cannot eat or even smell one.

On the other hand, I have equally powerful memories of great experiences, memories that I can't help but recall in conversation and fondly recount the wonderful feelings they brought about. Many of these revolve around food and dining. I believe this is because so many of our senses are engaged when we are dining. Once I was visiting an Italian restaurant with some friends. I was young and still new to going out to dine at "nicer" places. One of our buddies happened to be the server, and I had never actually seen him in this role before.

As my friend walked us through the experience, I remember being completely captivated by his talent. He did not just read the specials; he colorfully described how the chef was preparing each dish using all of the sensory descriptions at his command. He performed all of the steps of service with intention and care. I could tell he was taking great pride in how he served us and in showing us his skills.

I have never forgotten that experience, and I often use it as an example when training staff members on their tableside manner. The dish that I had may not have been the best dish ever made, but I certainly felt it was. I had little choice after how incredibly well presented the whole experience was. The food was an essential part of this experience, but the X factor in this case was the genuine enthusiasm, pride and care my friend took in serving us. It was a moment I will never forget, and after that day, I not only returned to that restaurant many times over, but suggested my friend's service to anyone who was willing to go and try the place.

The Heart of Hospitality #4: Hospitality is entertaining.

Let me tell you a secret. This is a key distinction that the majority of businesses overlook, and understanding it is crucial to understanding the insights we will be discussing in later chapters.

We are not here to serve food. We are here to entertain.

That is not necessarily to say that we are expected to be our Guests' sole entertainment, but rather, we are expected to entertain them as though they were in our home, to which we have personally invited them. Could you imagine inviting someone to your home for a special occasion, and then, once they arrived, completely ignoring them, or worse, acting as if they were some type of imposition?

Yet all of us can recall a time at a restaurant when we have felt exactly that. Remember the little café down the street from my home? Each time I walked into the space, I felt that I was not supposed to be there. The person at the counter would inevitably stand there with no greeting whatsoever, never make eye contact while I was ordering, and act disinterested in being there at all. And I'm not talking just one person—this happened with pretty much the whole staff! I was invited there by virtue of the business being open, but I felt unwelcome the instant I arrived. After two to three tries, I gave up. That café is no longer in business. Big surprise.

At the other coffeehouse down the road, on the other hand, the moment I set foot in the place for the first time, I felt like I was being welcomed to an event held by a dear friend. I was introduced to coworkers as if they were friends or family and I instantly felt at home - a part of. It is likely no surprise that not only do I go out of my way (and right past the old café) to visit, I highly recommend it to all of my friends.

A Sound Investment

Now that we understand what is meant by true hospitality, it's time to turn our attention to why it matters. What do emotion, personal connection, and sincere entertainment have to do with our bottom line?

The role of hospitality in business is often overlooked and certainly underutilized, even in the hospitality business itself. Yet it plays a vital role in turning our Guests into raving fans using only the resources within the walls of our establishments. Without this key ingredient, much of the benefit of our business acumen, promotional strategies, and hard work will eventually fall flat.

I find it helpful to think about this in terms of investing. People have so very many choices regarding where to invest their time, money, and life experiences. In this climate, how are we to ensure that Guests choose our business over and over again? The answer is, like any other investment. As long as we continue to pay dividends, people will continue to invest.

Let's think about that: If I put one thousand dollars into a stock, I am expecting that I will get a decent percentage return on top of that investment. If the investment nets me, say, ten percent, I may consider reinvesting in that stock. If I then make ten percent more, and the interest begins to compound, I may consider staying in longer. As long as that investment continues to pay off, I will continue to reinvest over time. Yet the minute there is a sharp downturn and I risk losing money, I may consider pulling out. If the company begins to falter and things look bleak, I will likely pull my energy away from that company and look towards another investment altogether.

We must understand that the moment a Guest comes in contact with our business, they have begun to invest in us. It is key to remember that they are not only investing their money, but also their time, their emotions, and their chance of having a positive, enriching experience—all things they will not be able to get back once they have bought in. These intangible things are much more valuable than cash. And if the energy that our Guests are putting into visiting us becomes a losing proposition, even on one visit, they will think twice about investing again.

We must also consider that for a Guest, the beginning of that investment could be little more than a phone call, an email inquiring about our products and services, or simply that first step through the front door. As soon as that connection is made, we are now in charge of their investment.

While on vacation recently, my wife and I visited a beautiful restaurant nestled in the hills of Napa California, owned by a dear friend of mine. This restaurant offers sweeping views of the mountains and hosts special events of all shapes and sizes, with nightly entertainment and award-winning cuisine from a renowned chef. The experience is truly like none other. Special occasions are celebrated there and it is considered somewhat of a destination restaurant. The hosts are trained to understand that no Guest should ever be turned away, despite the fact that the dining room is often booked solid with reservations. If a host cannot find space in the dining room for someone who has walked in without a reservation, they are instructed to alert management immediately. Managers will almost always find a creative solution to make sure the Guest has the option to dine, whether it be outside on the beautiful patio, or in the spacious lounge or bar area.

The main reason for this is that the restaurant is not a place that people likely just stumbled into. The Guest, whoever they are, made a decision to come and experience what this establishment has to offer. The very fact that they have traveled there, sometimes from miles away, means they had an intention and are excited to be there. Perhaps they have heard things from their friends about the space, or perhaps they are there to celebrate something special, but did not make a reservation ahead of time.

But there are also those who did just drive by, catch a glimpse of the stunning champagne chandeliers peeking through the twenty-foot windows or hear the music spilling from over the rooftop, and decide to check it out. Regardless of how or why they have come, simply by showing up, the Guest has now invested a part of their life into the business. At this point, it is the team's responsibility to begin paying dividends on that investment.

If for any reason it is physically impossible to accommodate a Guest due to sheer lack of space, a manager will personally arrange a reservation at a sister restaurant nearby. He will often arrange a special appetizer or dessert as well as a sign of gratitude for their interest in the restaurant.

By taking special care to seat everyone who arrives, this particular Napa restaurant showcases their understanding that they respect and value these Guests' investment of time, energy and emotion. They are connecting with those Guests and showing them that simply because they walked in the door, they are important. In doing so, they've already made a powerful impact, and those Guests are already more likely to return to the establishment and recommend it to their friends.

Trust is the Currency

If we continue thinking of this in terms of investment, we will want to begin paying dividends to our Guests right away. If so, what is the currency that we are expected to use? We obviously do not want to start giving them free product the moment they walk in the door. After all, we are still in business to make money, not just to make friends.

Yet I'd like you to consider that money, like everything else, is energy. In this investment model, we must begin to see our relationship with our Guests and with each other as pure energy. In order to entice people to spend their energy, and thus their money, with us, we must immediately begin to create a field of trust.

This may sound hokey, but bear with me. When people come together, an energetic bond begins to form. The energy we are sending toward one another will determine the quality of that bond. A bond that initially feels good to both parties can develop into a relationship of mutual faith. If two people or a group of people begin to trust each other, they will freely exchange energy among themselves. However, if those same people begin to distrust, they will quickly defend themselves and close off the flow of energy, retreating to find others that they are more able to trust. They will come to resent paying for services and end transactions as quickly as possible.

This currency of trust undergirds every monetary transaction that happens with our establishments. If trust and positive energy are flowing, money and opportunity will be shared more often, more freely, and without tension. In order to keep the flow of energy, and thus, the currency, moving between us and our Guests, we must continue to engage the relationship in a way that constantly reinforces that level of confidence.

One of the best examples I have seen of this is a Team Member I once worked with named Sheehan. Sheehan was a polished professional manager with a very dry sense of humor. It was sometimes difficult to know if he was serious or joking, which could make for some awkward and yet funny moments when working with him. One thing that Sheehan cared most about was making sure that when people entered the dining room they were greeted warmly and welcomed as if they were coming into his own home. No matter what he was doing when a Guest walked into his vicinity, he would stop to look them in the eye, often sticking out his hand and simply saying, "welcome."

If given the opportunity, he would offer, "My name is Sheehan, I am one of the managers. Please let me know if there is anything you need while you're here."

It may come as no surprise to learn that Sheehan became quite popular among the locals. In part, this was because his actions, from the moment he first came in contact with any Guest, created massive amounts of trust. By simply offering his assistance and genuine friendship right off the bat, people knew that if there was an issue Sheehan would be there to help them solve it. It should also come as no surprise that as the wine director, Sheehan was able to sell quite a lot of wine, thereby turning the currency of trust into cash.

From the Heart

In being of service, we transcend the doing and we inhabit the being. That is to say, true hospitality is less about what we do and more about who we are. He who has a heart of hospitality is a true ambassador. He is the host of the party, the master of ceremonies, ready to entertain as though this were his own home. He's never seen simply sitting in the wings. He is constantly in the mix, engaging deeply with all who are present. He works hard to build strong systems that everyone can rely on with the goal that he will be able to spend more time where he is most valuable: with his Guests.

This is someone who has a sincere desire to deliver heartfelt service to others. For this person, sincerity is a given: going through the motions, reading the script or doing just enough to get by will never do. Simply providing great service will never be enough, for he is on a crusade to win the hearts of those he serves.

A true steward of hospitality understands how to tap into emotion. She knows that people are driven by emotion. Spending habits, life decisions and behaviors are heavily influenced by whatever emotional state we happen to be in. By tapping into and creating heightened positive emotions, we invite our Guests to receive an uplifting experience that they will regularly return for.

Those who are serious about delivering true hospitality understand how to build personal relationships. When people feel that they have a personal connection they begin to put their faith and trust into the organization. Our Guests are far more likely to return when they feel they are a part of what we are doing on a greater level. They will want to bring their friends and family to be take part in what is going on there. They will want more and more of what we offer, and they will happily invest their time, money and energy where they feel most connected.

Chef Deborah Scott is one of the most amazing examples of delivering true hospitality I have seen. Having grown up in southeastern Virginia, she's no stranger to southern hospitality. When she made the trek to Southern California and set up shop with her first restaurant, she began doing what she instinctively knew to do. Rather than spending all of her time in the kitchen, she would regularly go out into the dining room and greet Guests as they dined. With a cheerful greeting of "how y'all doing tonight?" she began making friends with any and everyone who came to try her food. If a Guest had a special request, she would fly back to the kitchen and whip up something completely unique for them to try.

One Guest at a time, Chef Deb has slowly and steadily built a huge following. Each new restaurant she opens seems to become an instant success. By focusing more on those she serves than even her own food, she has become a local icon.

To this day, when you visit one of her restaurants, you will likely find Chef Deb floating from table to table, chatting it up with Guests and continuing to build personal relationships with each of them. The staff often affectionately quips "everyone knows Chef Deb." Even if you have only met her once, she has the ability to make you feel as though she is a trusted friend.

When was the last time you saw a chef present in the dining room in this way? It simply does not happen. But imagine the impact this would have on the experience. Imagine how you would feel if the executive chef of a restaurant came out to ask how you were enjoying things. This simple way of being has translated into a restaurant empire for Chef Deborah Scott, and it has also transformed the landscape of dining in Southern California.

Trudging the Road

Once we are armed with the understanding of how hospitality goes above and beyond service, and how the X factor plays into our business, we must now go out and execute it. Some days, this will feel arduous, and, in the face of everything else we must also do as leaders, we may be tempted to allow hospitality to take a backseat to other tasks. However, that would be straying down the wrong path. We must resist the urge not to put hospitality first at all times.

With so many things that go into ensuring proper execution in the restaurant, it is easy to be blinded by the moment-to-moment activities that must take place. There are many moving parts that must be synced carefully and efficiently for things to go right. People must work in a highly coordinated fashion, and efficient systems must be created and followed to ensure success.

It is easy to see why, in the face of all of this, it can become difficult to focus on and employ the X factor. Sometimes just getting from point A to point B requires the bulk of our energy. This is exactly why hospitality must become less of something we apply and more of something that we are. It requires us to begin seeing our businesses as less of a profit margin and more of an extension of who we are as our best selves. In order to do so, we must conquer the barrier imposed by the technical aspects of our businesses. In the next chapter, we'll explore the challenges they pose, and how to overcome them and allow our core values and true personalities to shine through.

The Bottom Line

When we are putting in the work to operate our businesses as an extension of our best selves, the characteristics of hospitality will naturally flourish. This is when the magic happens. Guests will feel a genuine sense of trust and welcome when they step into our establishments, and they will be delighted to invest their time, their energy, their emotions, and yes, their money, into us.

And, once hospitality is truly a part of our culture, we will begin to see the compounded results of these efforts in dividends that take many forms, including, but not limited to, pure profit.

CHAPTER TWO

AN INSIDE JOB

"In an age when so many groups are rolling out restaurants faster than a baker makes donuts, my goal is that each restaurant feels hand crafted. That they have their own soul." – Danny Meyer

---

Dr. Wayne Dyer, one of my very favorite authors and speakers, once told a story of a man who lost his keys inside his house during a power failure. The man groped around on the floor in the darkness for a long time, but couldn't find his keys. Then he noticed that, way down the block, a streetlight was on. So he left his house, went down the street, and started looking for his keys under the streetlight.

After a while, his neighbor saw him, and went over to see if he could help.

"What's wrong?"

"I dropped my keys."

"Where did you drop them?"

"In my living room."

"Then why are you looking for them under this streetlight?"

"Because the light's so much better out here!"

I get calls all the time from potential clients who are seeking a solution to a specific problem. Namely, how can they get more butts in seats, more often? When I ask them what they are currently doing to accomplish their goals, I often hear things like: "We are running ads on Facebook, Yelp and local food publications." "We changed our menus to include more options." "We are trying a late-night happy hour to boost after-dinner sales."

While these and other advertising and promotions solutions may be worthwhile, they can be like placing a band-aid on a gaping wound if there are other problems occurring inside the business. As owners, we might find ourselves in a situation similar to the man looking for his lost keys outside under the streetlight. Before we can consider the right type of outside solution—whether it be a promotion, advertisement or sales technique—we must first assess the health and vitality of certain aspects of our businesses to ensure we are operating on solid ground to begin with. In effect, our success is an inside job.

Under the Hood

This may seem obvious to the seasoned restaurateur, but no inside job would be complete without going over the importance of the critical systems that must be managed regularly if the business is to succeed at all. Whenever I am first introduced to a business, I will want to look at financials, systems, written policies, and various proprietary information in order to get a sense of the company's overall health.

After all, it is all well and good to talk about going above and beyond, about fostering a spirit of true hospitality and connecting with Guests on an emotional level, but how do we do this when we are bogged down in the daily grind it takes to run a business? The fact is, before we as management can focus our energy on creating an amazing experience that will leave our Guests raving, we have to ensure that our businesses are functioning smoothly on a day-to-day basis. That is what the inside job is all about.

As owners and managers, just as if we were keeping that vintage sports car in mint condition, we need to constantly be, not simply peeking under the hood every so often, but working on each component to keep it clean, finely tuned and operating at peak levels. When left unattended, parts become worn, systems fail, and we find ourselves paying a hefty repair bill or scrapping the thing altogether.

Bear with me if this is old hat, but I would suggest you use this chapter as a check on how well you or your teams are truly managing the systems in your business. Taking a good look at our businesses from an analytical point of view can tell us a lot. After all, results are what we are graded on, and looking at these systems provides a measurable way to visualize the results. Depending on what our specific goals are, these factors are what will determine whether we are ultimately able to sell for a maximum offer, grow and expand, or otherwise become more profitable.

It has always been surprising to me how few owners and managers truly take the time to build effective systems that will enable their businesses to grow. Over the years, I have found that this is due to several predictable, yet easily curable factors.

For this book, I will not go into great detail about the basic systems needed for a business to function, but I will mention some key components of certain vital aspects that often get overlooked. I come across these issues so often that I feel they are important to understand. First, I will present you with common stumbling blocks that prevent growth, and next I will offer a set of tried-and-true systems designed to help manage these and similar issues.

Stumbling Block #1: Lack of knowledge

Many people get into the restaurant business with no real operational experience to speak of. In many ways this can actually work in their favor, as these people may not be bound to arbitrary standards that the industry has dictated as "how things should be." Being free of some of these constraints can allow for innovation and creativity.

But there are also certain industry standards that are tried and true. To name a select but impactful few: effective systems of inventory, cost controls, and labor management are all crucial to success. If owners and managers do not have a thorough understanding of how these systems relate to profitability, there is a serious problem at hand. In that case, it is imperative that we educate ourselves and our teams on how to implement and manage these and other systems on a daily basis.

For example, take my client Allison. Allison runs a successful juicery with several locations and is profitable by industry standards, posting a consistent sixteen percent net profit across all stores, give or take the season. At first glance, those numbers might indicate that her business is on autopilot, poised for further growth. However, a look at her systems told a different story.

When Allison came to me to ask that I take a look at her operation, she shared that while things were going well financially, she was actually spending a ton of time running from store to store to buy bananas or napkins every time they ran out. She did not know exactly what her margins were, as she did not regularly review her financials and was not proficient with P&L (profit and loss).

With a systematic approach, I found that Allison simply lacked the knowledge of how to use vital information to make informed decisions that would affect the success and growth of her business. To solve this problem together, I began by coaching her through the process of reading and analyzing her daily reporting and profit and loss statements, then helping her to become more comfortable with costing and labor controls. As she grew more confident, she began finding new ways to become more efficient, curb waste and increase profit. All that required was some consistent focus on the areas that can bring the greatest results.

Stumbling Block #2: Lack of Bandwidth

Another factor that contributes to a lack of overall growth, and one I have seen all too often, is a business that has systems in place but cannot effectively manage them due to lack of bandwidth. At times, we are simply so busy putting out fires that the day-to-day management of critical components of our businesses can fall by the wayside.

It is true that we are always busy. The question is, busy doing what? We must constantly reorient ourselves around the activities that will ultimately bring the best results, lest we resign ourselves to spinning our wheels.

As a young general manager, I took on every task myself, feeling that I had to actually perform the task in order to understand it and execute it properly. After a year or so of working this way, I burned out. I had no idea that I was becoming more and more ineffective as I took on more and more. I accepted the idea that the job was simply overwhelming and continued on, despite the negative ramifications to my health and relationships. Noticing my state, and concerned that I might falter under the weight of everything I was taking on, a trusted mentor of mine pointed out the need for me to begin to learn the value of one simple word: *delegate*.

It took me a while to feel comfortable letting go of some of the tasks that I thought were absolutely necessary for me to perform, but once I started to empower others to take these tasks on, some amazing things happened. For one, I became free to focus on the most important aspects of the job: Guest-facing activities rather than office-related tasks. I learned that the general manager's time was far better spent developing relationships and becoming active in the community at large than on tasks that required a lot of time and energy but were not necessarily contributing to the direct growth of the business.

I also learned that when I put faith and trust in those under my direction, they took the opportunity to learn and grow in their positions, which ultimately created a far more productive and positive work environment for them. This was a particularly impressive side effect of learning to delegate. We will discuss more on this topic in Chapter Three.

Like I once had, Allison found this concept particularly tough to embrace, as she was used to operating so many aspects of the business herself and had trouble finding someone she could trust to handle problems as they arose the way she would. For many of us, this can be one of the scariest aspects of growing our business. Sadly, many of us will actually sacrifice the growth rather than let go of the reins and trust others to rise up. This leads us to our next factor.

Stumbling Block #3: Lack of Training

To set ourselves up for growth, we must concede that the best way to ensure our success is to surround ourselves with others who know more than we do in particular areas. Letting go of the reins can be tough, but when partnerships are carefully created and maintained, we can leverage the power of others' knowledge for massive growth. And while sometimes this looks like finding experts with the knowledge that we need, as owners and management we can also cultivate the knowledge needed by allowing staff we already have to grow. Training staff is another invaluable way to let go of the reins and refocus our own energy where it will be most effective. And by taking the time to share our knowledge and carefully cultivate our staff's growth, we are also directly growing our businesses. It all comes down to one phrase that I use in all of my training: "Grow the People, Grow the Business."

In Allison's case, we implemented a training program for store leaders with incentives to perform and hold others accountable, which improved the Team Member and Guest experience at her juiceries. By setting up a system of *how to*'s and *how not to*'s, we were able to take much of the running around off Allison's plate, in many cases eliminating the need altogether. Not only that, she began to define a clear culture of staff growth, which then started to attract top talent through word of mouth. Her problem of never being able to find reliable staff started to change. She began filling her roster with rock stars, making her job not only easier, but far more enjoyable.

For a quick recap on the most common problems that I see holding businesses back from growth, let's return to Allison's larger situation. Remember that Allison wanted to expand into more markets but could not manage to find the cashflow to do so. She had been very successful with her first few stores, reinvesting capital back into the business, but she seemed to hit a wall now that her business had grown, and she felt like she was spread too thin.

After spending a few days working in her stores, I could quickly see that Allison did not have systems in place that could allow her to control her business and ease her workflow while simultaneously training her amazing team to do the same. At that point, she lacked the knowledge of basic systems, time and energy to focus on growth, and the ability to train her staff to support her.

Over the next few months, Allison and I were able to work on these issues. We installed a simple yet effective system of inventory for her business that allowed us to detect and eliminate good deal of wasteful practices, saving hundreds per week in product and improving her food cost. We also tweaked her scheduling to allow for most effective Team Members to be in the store during peak hours and to maximize productivity while saving an average of $60 per day per store in labor. With annual revenues per store around $800,000, this resulted in just under 3% in labor savings alone! Combined with the training program for store leaders mentioned above, which vastly improved the Team Member and Guest experience, these changes set Allison up for further growth. She has recently opened her fifth store and is showing no signs of stopping!

The same fixes that helped Allison can help many of us who are struggling to achieve a position in which growth is possible; I'll go into some of them below. When we have systems in place to help manage these fundamentals, we will have a strong foundation on which to build incredible marketing momentum from within our own businesses.

Essential Ingredients for Success

A friend of mine, Tom, contacted me one day and announced that he had opened a restaurant. I had known Tom for several years, and I knew that he had never been in the business before, although he had been quite successful in sales and marketing. I must have looked at him like he was crazy, because he promptly told me that he had no idea what he was doing and was looking for someone to help him. Knowing that he was quite a brilliant businessman, I understood that what he meant was he desired knowledge of how to set up and execute the internal systems that he would need in order to scale his business quickly, which was his goal. Tom, like many entrepreneurs, is an "idea guy." He knows how to dream big, and he makes it his business to surround himself with those who have the knowledge and expertise to execute those ideas. Excited to become a part of helping his vision, I signed on to help him build those systems, and then to train others how to manage them as the company grew.

In the next section, I will outline a similar set of systems to the ones I helped Tom build for his business. These are basics; they are not unique to any one outfit, but are certainly essential in order to build a strong foundation for future growth. These basics consists of inventory, recipe costing, and labor costing.

Essential Systems #1: Inventory

Here is one simple fact: Some of you reading this book are not taking a regular inventory within your business. I guarantee you, this will end up losing you money.

Simply stated, in the restaurant industry, we sell product. That product is made up of multiple ingredients. Each day, food and beverage is delivered into our stores and prepared to sell. Every can of tomatoes, every carrot, every bottle of wine represents a small component of all that we sell. Every single ounce of these products makes up our inventory, as we continuously hold these products while they are being prepared to sell. If these are not accounted for on a regular basis, we will not have an accurate picture of how cash is flowing in and out of our business.

Inventory can be accounted for on a monthly, weekly or even daily basis, depending on the volume of business we are engaged in. For incredibly busy operations, it may not make sense to take a daily inventory, as this requires quite a lot of people power. Often, however, for businesses that are struggling to account for their product, I recommend a more frequent inventory, at least until things can get under control. One thing is for certain: If you are not taking regular inventory of your product, you are absolutely losing money. It really does not matter if you use a web-based system or something as simple as Excel. Inventory must be done, and it must be accurate.

One friend of mine, a chef, was sharing with me the challenge he faced taking over a new restaurant as executive chef. The staff was taking regular inventory, but they were not doing so accurately. When counting steaks, the team would estimate how much they thought was on the shelf, rather than actually weighing the product. The total inventory being reported each month was generally off by at least $11,000 one way or another. In a scenario like this, it was impossible for my friend to know how much profit was actually made, if any.

Again, to the seasoned pro, this seems glaringly obvious, but you would be as shocked as I am to see how many owners are not taking accurate inventory—and how many are not doing it at all.

For those who struggle with this, I recommend starting simply. Following the practices in the list below will help streamline an inventory system and avoid the major pitfalls I see all too often.

1. Make sure that all of the pricing of each product you receive is up to date and accurate.

2. Be sure that the amount you measure for each product is also accurate. Is it a ten-ounce portion that you are counting? A twelve-ounce can? Or a box containing forty units of the product? Be sure the pricing matches the unit of measure.

3. Keep your inventory well organized. Storing things haphazardly creates waste. You may be ordering product you think you don't have when it is just hiding behind the tomatoes. Perishables can also go to waste if not rotated and stored properly.

4. Organize your inventory "sheet-to-shelf" to make things easy to count. Your inventory count sheets should match what is on the shelf as much as possible. This makes it very easy to count product as you go, moving through your kitchen and storage spaces.

5. Use two people to count inventory. I like to have one person "spotting" and another recording the numbers. This will help create fewer mistakes and move things along more efficiently.

6. Double-check the numbers. Once you have input inventory into your accounting program, make sure pricing, units of

measure and actual counts are accurate. If something looks off, go back and check to see where the mistake may have been made.

If you are painstaking about this process, you will undoubtedly begin to see immediate results that translate into increased confidence in operational decisions and a healthier bottom line.

Essential Systems #2: Recipe Costing

Another area that I find to be a challenge, especially for busy operators, is proper costing of menu items. Each item on our menu has a specific *recipe cost*, that is, the cost it takes to produce the dish. Let's say you are serving a roasted sea bass with herb polenta and asparagus. Every ingredient that goes onto that plate has a specific cost attached.

Perhaps the sea bass itself is an eight-ounce portion. If you are paying $16 per pound, that eight-ounce portion would cost eight dollars. Four stalks of asparagus may cost another $0.75. The polenta, sauce and any garnish may add another dollar to the plate. So now, the plate cost is $9.75. If our goal is to attain a twenty-five percent food cost, that is, the cost of producing the dish is twenty-five percent of what we would sell it for, then the price of the dish would need to be $39.

Now let's say our market would not allow us to charge $39 for that dish. Who would feel comfortable paying that much for a piece of fish? This is where we need to use the tools of recipe costing to inform our menu and management decisions. Here are some things we could do to improve our results:

1. Compare pricing across different vendors. I am very loyal to my vendors, but will always research to make sure I am getting the best product for the best price. Not doing so could cost us quite a bit, especially if I can buy the same product for less elsewhere.

2. Play with the portions on the plate. Creating a beautiful dish and using smart accompaniments and garnishes can create a lot of perceived value for very little cost.

3. Cross-utilize product. The less dish-specific items we hold in our inventory, and the more ingredients we can use across multiple dishes, the more efficient we are, and the less waste we create.

4. Be aware of loss leaders. We may want to serve some high-end dishes on our menu that net a much smaller margin, but other dishes can make up for this loss. For instance, we may serve a high-end steak that results in a thirty-eight percent food cost for the dish, but we also serve some fried calamari or another popular appetizer with only a twelve percent food cost.

At the end of the day, if we are balancing out to our goal of twenty-five percent, we can offer valuable items to our Guests and meet our goals at the same time. As an added measure, by focusing on selling more of those items that capture a higher margin, we can effectively lower our food cost significantly.

Essential Systems #3: Labor Costing

Like the cost of the product we sell, the cost of labor is a prime controllable, and for that reason it must be managed daily, if not hourly. One huge mistake I see operators make all the time is to schedule labor and then fail to control it throughout the shift. Paying attention to business levels, managing tasks, and leveraging Team Member skillsets can contribute to saving hundreds, if not thousands of dollars.

Yet many operators leave these things to chance by not focusing enough on them daily. If you are currently in this boat, here is a list of best practices and common fixes I recommend to everyone. Considering and implementing these options will set you on a path for future growth:

1. Schedule to a budget.

Often, schedules are made to accommodate the needs of the job without taking into consideration the budgeted goal for labor. For instance, we may need six servers on a Saturday night. If service starts at 5 PM, you may have those servers come in at 4 PM to get ready for the shift. The server assistants may come in at 4:30 PM, food runners at 4:45 PM and hosts at 4 PM and 5 PM. Such a schedule certainly may accommodate the needs of the restaurant— sometimes. Yet depending on the actual sales volume the restaurant is producing on a given night, we may not be making our labor goals.

Let's say our goal for front-of-house labor is ten percent. If, when making our schedules, we are keeping in mind our projected sales based on historical data, we may find that we are grossly overscheduling our staff compared to our labor goal. It may be that we can stagger clock-in times to adjust to busier times of the evening, eliminate a position for a certain shift, or otherwise adjust to better meet our goal. It may also be okay to run a higher labor cost on Mondays if we know that a busy Saturday will balance costs out for the week.

Either way, we must be mindful of our budget in order to make informed, efficient decisions when scheduling. If we are not using a budget to schedule, we are flying blind and hoping for the best— an easy way to lose when it gets to the bottom line.

2. Cut staff quickly when business is slow.

It is very easy for a manager to get a little complacent and allow staff to work through the shift and leave whenever their work is done. However, a dutiful manager will stay on top of the shift, make sure people continue working efficiently, and cut those who are no longer needed for the day. They will also follow up to make sure that tasks are finished quickly and the Team Members move along to get off of the clock.

3. Leverage high-value Team Members.

It's always a smart idea to "keep aces in places," that is, to use the most effective Team Members when and where they best serve the business's needs. A server who is highly motivated and consistently shows high sales may be best scheduled on the busiest shifts. A line cook who is also a rock star at prep might be put in charge of overseeing prep operations just before or during the regular shift to improve efficiency overall.

By utilizing these great Team Members, not only will we improve the operation, we will show them that they are appreciated, making them more likely to continue to invest their energy in our business

4. Cross-train every department.

In my restaurants, I find it incredibly useful to cross-train staff across all departments. Servers who attain proficiency at bartending not only feel empowered by learning a new skill, they become incredibly more valuable to the team as a whole. Line cooks who know how to work every station are very useful in times when someone does not show, if cuts are made, and when the skill is needed in more than one area. I encourage food runners to learn kitchen skills and hosts to train as cocktail servers. Providing pathways to advancement is great for the team and can save quite a bit of money in the end.

The Bottom Line

In case you are wondering what all of this has to do with creating raving fans who cannot wait to come back again and again, consider this: Unless we have a firm grasp on the basics and our operations are running as effectively and as profitably as possible to begin with, we will have no foundation on which to build. For the business to survive, the very basic functions listed above must not only be present, but managed and monitored daily.

For the owner-operator, these basic but crucial systems can easily become sidelined by the perils of the day-to-day grind. Putting out fires and simply minding the shop can be overwhelming enough. Finding the extra energy needed to manage the numbers can be a tall order after a long day. "I will get to it tomorrow" can stretch out for days, weeks, months.

This can become a dangerous downward spiral. Before we know it, we have lost control of the basics, and we are caught in the trap that so many of us have found ourselves in: We have created a job for ourselves that we never wanted when we first opened our business. Even more distressing, finding the money to hire someone to do it for us can seem impossible. The margins might be too thin, and we might tell ourselves that if we can just work a little harder and bring in a little more business, then we will earn enough to hire help.

Does any of this sound familiar? Trust me. You are not alone. Most if not all businesses have gone through something similar.

 Many of you are likely familiar with Michael Gerber's books *The E-Myth* and *The E-Myth Revisited*, which brilliantly illustrate the power of working *on* our businesses versus working *in* our businesses. By carefully and diligently building systems, then training others how to manage those systems, we are more aptly able to go about the business of growing the business. Yet understanding these principles and putting them into action are two very different scenarios.

To remedy this, often all that is required is a shift in mindset. Consider this quote by T. Harv Ecker, author of the bestselling book *Secrets of the Millionaire Mind: Mastering the Inner Game of Wealth*. "Where attention goes, energy flows and results show."

By shifting our focus to the activities that produce the greatest results, we can leverage much of the energy currently reserved in our days for mundane, although necessary, tasks. It is this fundamental shift in energy that will allow us to build the foundation upon which all of our dreams can be built.

No procedure will yield any type of real result unless we are highly effective at managing the systems we have in place. However, systems are nothing without the people who run them. Ultimately, that is what the bulk of this book is aimed at exploring: the people. The people we serve and the people we employ.

Now that we've discussed the basics required for a solid foundation, in the following chapter, we will explore the role of the people behind the systems—and the people the systems are built to serve. This is the next step in building an unshakeable service model designed to support a steady flow of butts in seats.

CHAPTER THREE

YOUR UNSHAKABLE SERVICE MODEL

"At JW Marriott, how we treat our Guests starts with how we treat each other. That is the JW Marriott treatment." – JW Marriott

Every business has a handful of clients who are considered VIP. Perhaps they are the people who spend the most money at our business; perhaps they are the people with whom we've developed deep and special relationships. Regardless of the motivation, we all know those particular Guests we would bend over backwards for. When one of these people shows up as we are about to close the doors for the day, we open them willingly and invite them in. If they have a special need or request, we accommodate it without question, as if they were a member of our own family. If they mistakenly leave without paying a bill, we shrug it off and trust that we will see them again to settle up. We give these people every ounce of leeway and every benefit of the doubt, because in our eyes, they are special in some way. We simply treat them like royalty.

Yet there are other Guests who do not necessarily enjoy the same spoils. The doors do not swing open as readily for these people. We are a bit quicker to decline certain requests. Our internal systems do not have VIP marked next to their names to alert our staff when they arrive. This does not mean that we treat them poorly, but they are clearly in a different class. They may or may not get that extra-special treatment when they arrive. Their experience is left more to chance, depending on the day.

The same can be said for our Team Members. In fact, it is not uncommon in the workplace for certain Team Members to receive preferred treatment over others. Some Team Members may feel marginalized, or unappreciated, or as if they are just going through the motions on any given day. It should come as no surprise that many people see their jobs as a means to an end: a duty that they are obligated to perform in order to earn money to pay bills, but certainly not a source of joy and fulfillment. Team Members who don't fit into the VIP category are certainly more likely to feel this way about their jobs.

In most places, this kind of system, where some people are valued more than others, is status quo. Now, I invite you to consider what might happen it that were not the case.

What if each and every one of our Guests *and* our Team Members were treated like a VIP?

What if the doors swung open with a smile as each Team Member entered the building for work that day? What if each day, Team

Members came to work on fire to tackle the next project, excited to contribute to the team, and confident in their abilities to grow the business? What if they knew that opportunity was lurking at every corner, and the rewards of a job well done were theirs to claim? How productive and efficient would our operations become with individuals like these in charge of each department? How would each Guest feel when they entered the business as they were greeted by these champions of our cause?

Our Best Guests

In this chapter, we will shift our focus from avoiding getting bogged down by mundane tasks to *working on* our businesses. In order to take the next steps toward attaining the freedom that is necessary to effectively grow our businesses, we must make an effort to cultivate the culture by focusing on the people we serve. And in order to understand how to treat every Guest like a VIP, we must understand that the people we serve also include our Team Members.

I have always believed that my Team Members are my best Guests. They are the ones on the front lines, delivering the message and creating relationships even when I am not there. I could not reasonably expect them to act as I would in any given situation if I do not model for them the behavior I expect, and I cannot expect them to believe in our overall goals unless they are engaged in the process. It is not until we have achieved the goal of Team Member engagement that we can get to the business of delighting our Guests.

It is important to point out that there is a difference between Team Member *satisfaction* and Team Member *engagement*. Satisfaction is the metric that is typically used to measure how happy a Team Member is at their job. If we provide healthcare, flexible hours, good pay, and other benefits, it is likely that our Team Members will report being "satisfied" with their job. And that is not a bad thing.

But being "satisfied" is entirely different from being productive, and certainly falls short of the goal of "being on fire for creating amazing experiences for our Guests." For a Team Member to exhibit this type of engagement, there must exist a commitment to an atmosphere of mutual purpose, mutual respect, and high levels of psychological ownership. In other words, they must have an ownership mentality.

Never underestimate the power of a happy, committed Team Member. Team Members who are invested in our businesses sincerely and wholeheartedly will contribute more, become more productive, and, ultimately, transfer massively positive energy to our Guests, both at work and in the community.

The Power of Words

You may have noticed some unusual capitalization choices in this book, especially as we begin discussing the people we serve—both those who consume our products and services, and those who help us provide them. In case this seems unconventional or confusing, I invite you to consider the following.

One of my partners refuses to call a bar towel a rag. He feels it cheapens the tool and sets a different tone than does the word "towel." And while this may seem extreme to some, one important idea that I have learned over years of managing teams is this: Words matter. How we choose to express ourselves—that is, to present ourselves to the world—is very often how the world will perceive us.

While there are many factors that go into how we present ourselves, there are few that are as powerful and effective as the words we use. We can choose to use words that inspire, empower, or soothe; and we can express our words in a tone that allows them to be received in a certain way, for better or for worse. We can also choose to use words that are derogatory or defaming, again in a tone that can punctuate the true meaning behind them. These small changes can make a world of difference in the experience those around us have and the emotions they reflect back to us.

In my restaurants, we are obsessive about using the word "Guest" rather than "customer." Customer has always seemed so insincere and sets a marginalizing sort of tone. On the other hand, Guest is inviting and creates an air of humility that positions us to serve.

We also prefer to call our employees Team Members. Rather than sounding corporate and uncaring, this creates an inclusive, collaborative atmosphere—essential elements of a great culture. I chose to capitalize both words in this book to emphasize how important these distinctions are, and the fact that these people, our Guests and Team Members, are in many ways the heart and vitality of the restaurant industry. This is also the reason keeping them engaged is so crucial that I've devoted this chapter to the topic.

There are so many examples of how important words can be when building culture, but the point is simple: Words really do have power. If we are careful to choose those that support our mission, we can leverage one more often-overlooked but incredibly impactful tool to build a thriving business ecosystem—one that produces amazing results.

Emotions Matter

While most employers attempt to satisfy their Team Members with job-related benefits, it is often emotion-based personal relationships that lead to Team Members feeling more engaged— inspiring them to be more productive, more motivated, and more excited to become ambassadors of our brands.

When evaluating their level of engagement for themselves, Team Members will often ask themselves several clarifying questions. Questions such as, *Do I feel valued? Do I value the company that I work for? Do I belong?* If our Team Members do not feel that they are a part of a bigger picture, something larger than themselves, or if they do not understand how they contribute to the goals of the organization, they are more likely to disengage.

Disengagement is wasteful. Disengagement is unproductive. Disengagement leads to profit loss. Disengagement will not create raving fans.

The worst possible scenario is to have Team Members who are not just actively disengaged, but disgruntled or irritated. If a Team Member or a group of Team Members has gotten to this point, a cancer exists within the organization. Unfortunately, often, by the time owners or management recognize this kind of problem, much of the damage has already been done. Cleaning up a mess like this is frustrating, tedious and costly, but it can and must be done.

Fortunately, we can prevent such a hassle by recognizing it and employing several critical requirements that will create strong Team Member engagement. When these ingredients are implemented and practiced regularly, we will then create a culture that is guaranteed to create raving fans who return again and again. You will want to evaluate the current condition of your culture to be sure these elements exist and plan to make them a non-negotiable part of your management process. In my view, there are three critical requirements for creating Team Member engagement: leading by example, providing feedback both positive and negative, and offering opportunities for growth. In the next section, we'll dive into those in detail.

Critical Requirement of Team Member Engagement #1: Lead with the Broom

One day, I was visiting my favorite taco shop, which has several locations around town, when I noticed a handsome young gentleman sweeping around the tables. Quite frankly, he looked slightly older than the usual high-school-to-college-age-Team Member. He just seemed so happy to be there as he swept and spoke to the staff in a directive, yet soft and friendly tone. I surmised that he must be more of the management type and so I struck up a conversation.

He introduced himself as the taco shop's founder, and I was pleased to have the opportunity to thank him for bringing this concept to our neighborhoods. I shared with him that the word on the street was they were not only known for their amazing product, but the best service around. I asked him what his secret was, adding that I was curious why he was spending his time in the store sweeping, as I was sure he had much more to do. His answer was simple yet profound.

"I am sweeping simply because it needs to be done. In our culture, we lead with the broom. When my staff sees me here doing things that need to be taken care of, it empowers them to do the same. No task is too small for any of us to accomplish, and if we are all pitching in and leading by example, it ultimately leads to a much better Guest experience."

The evidence to back up his statement is clear. Whenever I visit any of their locations, I am likely to find a clean, friendly, efficient experience.

I am not suggesting that owners and managers should be sweeping floors all day. However, when I am acting in a coaching or consulting role, I am always interested in whether my clients' leaders lead from the front. That is, by example.

Ask any Team Member which manager they would do anything for and they will tell you: They will happily follow the manager who is hands-on and in the trenches with them. Not only that, but they will do their best work for those managers even when they are not around. And that must always be our goal and benchmark as owners and managers: how well does the establishment run in our absence?

By leading with the broom, that is to say, setting an example as a supportive role model, we teach our Team Members that they are empowered to take action even on the little things. "That's not my job" does not exist in this kind of environment. And since it is, or at least should be, our goal to cultivate in our staff great leaders who will lead in our absence, this is a crucial element to setting a tone of empowerment for the business and keeping our Team Members fully engaged.

Critical Requirement of Team Member Engagement #2: Share the Love

Sharing the love can mean many things, but in this book, what I'm talking about is simple: feedback. For owners and management, giving feedback to our Team Members must happen constantly and consistently throughout each working day.

It is easy to get into the groove of a shift and become a slave to the grind. Providing steps of service, preparing dishes, handling schedules, filing reports, dealing with Guest or Team Member issues—all of it takes up time and energy. And let's face it, we have a finite amount of energy each day. Throughout the years, I have found that one thing tends to get lost in all of this: taking the time to provide Team Member feedback.

However, when feedback is pushed to the wayside, we are losing a critical element for keeping our Team Members engaged. And in fact, if we were to make this a top priority, many of the tasks mentioned above would become much easier to manage. Remember that people are motivated by emotion. Providing feedback on a regular basis cultivates confidence, which leads to empowerment and inspiration—powerful emotions that will drive your Team

Members to go the extra mile, treat Guests like VIPs and become brand ambassadors.

One way to share the love is through instructive coaching. I once had a chef who was having a hard time with one of his line cooks. Alex was great on the sauté station, but he had aspirations of mastering the broil. The broil station at this particular restaurant commanded all of the bragging rights for the line. It was the place that, if you were good, you would be certain to receive consistent accolades from management, servers and Guests. It was simply a rock star position, and Alex had greatness in his sights.

After several months of campaigning for the position, Alex's chance finally came. The star broil master moved on to another company. The chef approached Alex and let him know that this was his time to shine. He could hardly wait.

He took his post on a busy Friday night and proceeded to get beat to a pulp. Eight steaks came back cooked improperly within the first hour. As the tickets flew in and the pressure mounted, Alex crumbled under the weight. Nonetheless, he had another shot the next night to redeem himself. Once again, Alex struggled. And although he seemed to get a little better on some nights, several more shifts went by, and the chef became furious. The chef scolded Alex every night, and at the point I came in, he was ready to terminate him.

As I began to investigate, I found that throughout his weeks on the broil station, Alex had never been given any real feedback, coaching or training in the position. He had been given the chance and held accountable for the results, but he had never received the support and guidance necessary to succeed in the position. The chef was simply scolding Alex rather than actually giving feedback and instruction.

I asked the chef to give Alex two more weeks and instructed him to work side by side with him in an instructive way, giving him feedback on each skill. Alex would be allowed to make mistakes, but the chef would correct him as they went along and monitor his improvement. I also asked the chef to provide Alex with specific written goals for each week and to sit with him for five minutes after each shift to go over those goals and what he needed to see from him to advance to the next skill.

The feedback I received from both Team Members after the two weeks was encouraging. Both of them developed feelings of empowerment and confidence. Alex felt valued and encouraged to continue. He still made some mistakes along the way, but he showed improvement, and was promoted to sous chef several months later. Not only did Alex benefit from this, but the chef did as well. By taking the time to properly instruct a Team Member and share his knowledge and skillset, he became more engaged as a leader. Others around them saw this as well and began asking for similar coaching. The entire team was motivated by what they saw and the energy on the line shifted in a very positive way.

Sometimes sharing the love means sharing tough love. I recently took part in a management meeting where some comments about a particular Team Member came up. This server was described as having trouble with her position. She frequently showed up to work late, was not prepared to be on the floor in a timely manner, and consistently missed steps of service, leading to a few Guest complaints.

During this conversation, another manager chimed in to state that he was having similar issues with another Team Member. He began to complain about this Team Member's behavior and attitude. He said that it had been going on for quite some time and he was "over it." However, when I asked the team what had been done so far in terms of coaching and counseling these Team Members, I got crickets. One manager said, "Oh, I've told them they need to watch it, but nothing has changed." I asked the general manager if she had been aware of these issues and she sheepishly said, "No."

The problem here is that we have several Team Members who are not working up to standard, but they are not being given the opportunity to improve. I explained to the group that it is not okay for the management team to simply complain about a Team Member's performance when they have done nothing to actually coach that person to success.

Delivering tough love can be uncomfortable for some. This is one reason managers tend to avoid these types of conversations. They do not want to deal with conflict. Perhaps they feel too close to that Team Member to deliver that type of conversation. These kinds of discussions produce fear and anxiety, which many want to avoid. But when faced head-on and motivated by compassion and a sincere desire to help someone to improve, this tough love can also produce the emotions of acceptance and approval.

Sharing the love in any and all of its forms, when done consistently and with good intention, can be one of the most powerfully motivating gifts we can bestow upon our teams. Do yourself and the business a favor and make this a non-negotiable critical requirement for your leaders to employ.

Critical Requirement of Team Member Engagement #3: Shatter the Glass Ceiling

Once a Team Member feels they are at a dead end and there is no more opportunity for growth, she will begin looking for another position outside the company. At this point, we have lost her. She cannot see herself growing any further in the organization. To cease growing is to begin dying. A Team Member that has started down this dark path is disconnected, unproductive, and, at worst, can spread a cancerous negativity among the team.

I once had a Team Member whom here I will call Karen. She was hired as a host at an upscale fine-dining restaurant with some brief experience in a similar establishment prior. Karen was a sweet girl with a pleasant smile and seemed eager to do a great job. After several weeks in her position, however, nearly all of these qualities quickly declined. She seemed quite disinterested and disconnected at times. When she was coached, she would swear that she wanted to do a great job and was committed to doing her best. After a coaching session, she would often show improvement, but soon she would once again would veer off course.

One day, when passing by the host stand, I caught her rolling her eyes at a Guest. Fortunately, the Guest did not see this, but I did. I took Karen aside for a few moments and asked her what was going on. For someone who had such potential and seemed to really want to do well, she sure had a funny way of showing it when she was actually on stage. She began welling up in tears and shared with me that, though she had been afraid to let me know because I was her boss, she really did not like the position that she was in. She thought she would do better as a server assistant. I was a bit taken aback at this notion. My conception of her was not someone who would typically fit the mold of that position. Server assistants need to be quick, agile and full of energy. They need to be able to multitask and possess an upbeat type of energy that I just did not see in Karen. Nonetheless, I wanted to give her a chance, so we moved her to that department, with the understanding that we would need to see her shine right away if she was to continue working with us.

After a couple of days of training, Karen was on the floor and ready to show her stuff. And an amazing thing happened. Karen completely transformed into a spritely, nimble go-getter. She seemed happy and eager to perform. She quelled our doubts and exceeded our expectations. We had found her hidden strengths. Eventually, Karen worked her way into a bar-back position and later became an accomplished bartender. As our relationship developed over time, we laughed about those early days and she would often thank us for allowing her the chance to grow in a positive direction.

The example above is one where the Team Member did not necessarily see the opportunity in front of her. Sometimes a shift in mindset and the willingness to provide another opportunity, perhaps at another location within our own company, can turn this into a situation which benefits everyone. Most Team Members seek opportunity. When they feel there is none, some Team Members will seek it elsewhere—outside of the walls of our businesses. And sometimes that is truly what is best for that Team Member. Perhaps we do not have the right opportunity for them, but can somehow assist with advancement at another company.

The point is, if we always make it our mission to improve the personal and professional experience of our Team Members, they are more likely to feel trust and belonging, which leads to them becoming ambassadors for our brands. This is why shattering the glass ceiling by offering opportunity to our teams is a crucial requirement of Team Member engagement.

Great Expectations

Now that we have defined the three critical requirements for Team Member engagement, we can turn our attention to addressing what we know our Guests expect: the three critical requirements for Guest engagement. For the purpose of this chapter, these standards are the most basic and fundamental expressions of what our Guests need to experience if they are ever to consider investing with us again.

Understand that without this foundation, it will be difficult for you to employ the principles of hospitality which I share throughout the book in an effective manner. I suggest conducting a searching and deeply honest personal audit of how your business fares in each of the following areas, and if there is any room for improvement, begin working right away to shore up any issues.

Critical Requirement of Guest Engagement #1: Raise the Bar

In order to be considered viable, people must be able to trust the product that we produce. This of course means amazing food presented in an amazing way. But it also includes things like atmosphere, décor, the look and feel of the staff and the general mood of the establishment. All of the details must be tended to in order to give a remarkable overall Guest experience. This is a baseline standard. People expect much more out of their experience than the basics and instinctively know when the wool is being pulled over their eyes. Most will vote with their feet and never return with even the slightest of infractions.

A simple statement I use all the time can also be considered an incredibly powerful paradigm from which we should always be operating: *Details matter*. Details matter to our Guests, which means they should matter to us. If my wife reads this she may smack me, but I would consider her a person who has very high expectations when it comes to her environment and experience when dining. She's quite understanding when things go wrong, but will quickly cross an establishment off her list if they are not tending to the details. Her philosophy, like many diners', is that there are hundreds of other places that are willing to keep a high standard, so why not visit those instead?

This is perhaps the biggest challenge that we as owners and managers face in our industry today. If we are not fully and sincerely committed to providing an impeccable experience, then we will be left behind by the rest of the industry and certainly be seen as uncaring. And uncaring is not the label that we should seek among our peers and the public. By not tending to the details and committing to providing impeccable product, we are sending that exact message. Put simply, we must raise the bar for ourselves so that those we serve get *more* than they expected.

I once heard a story told by one of the greatest success coaches of all time, Tony Robbins. He was speaking about the standards we hold for ourselves, and he used his interaction with basketball star Michael Jordan as an example. Michael Jordan is arguably the best basketball player who ever lived. Yet most are not aware of what it took for him to claim that title. When Michael was in high school, he was cut from the varsity team.

It's also little known that Michael is quoted as saying this was one of the best things that could've ever happened for his career. His coach at the time told him that, despite his incredible natural talent, he was lacking the discipline and drive he needed in order to be a contributor to the team. He told Michael that if he wanted to be on the team next year, he would need to show up early to school every day, put in the hard work he needed to develop his studies in consistent effort, and then he could be on next year's roster. Michael worked hard that entire year, put in the effort each day, and was awarded his spot the following year. Of course, he did phenomenally well and became the star of the team. He raised his standard by improving his work ethic, and it paid off.

But once in the NBA, Michael Jordan's career did not explode until he experienced his next real challenge. His team had just lost the championship to Detroit and he found himself sitting at the back of the bus feeling devastated. He was wallowing in the defeat and having thoughts of blame towards other teammates for not having done their jobs, as well as feeling sorry for himself about the loss. Then he thought back to those days in high school and how he had overcome adversity back then by raising his standards.

That year, he worked harder than ever, practicing relentlessly, raising his personal standards to be the absolute best he could possibly be. He went on to win three NBA championships, and then, after a brief retirement, returned to win three more.

The defining factor here is that Michael was not competing with those around him. He was competing with himself. By raising the bar on his own expectations for himself, he was able to dominate the sport and make history. Of course, natural talent played a huge part in his success, but had he not set a standard for himself in those tough times, he may never have gotten to the point to let that talent shine.

If we are holding *ourselves* to a higher standard than even our Guests hold us to, we will always over-deliver. What a great way to begin the process of engaging our Guests by showing we care about the details that affect their experience!

Critical Requirement of Guest Engagement #2: Timely Service

When I was young, I would beg my mom to let me order a book or a game or some other fun toy from a mail-in catalog. These paper catalogs were magic to me. I could leaf through the pages, check the box to indicate which item I wanted to order, and have my mom write a check, which she would insert into the envelope to be mailed off. Once the envelope was in the mail, it was time to wait for four to six weeks for those mysterious forces to get to work and ensure that my package would someday arrive.

Today, it is hard to imagine having to wait even more than several days for something I have ordered to show up. We live in a world that enables us to make our choices and get instant gratification. The other day, I was speaking with my best friend. He told me that the strap on his daughter's backpack had broken and he'd needed to replace it right away. A trip to Target would seem like the natural solution, but instead he chose Amazon. One click later, a brand-new backpack was delivered to his doorstep—within two hours. He never even had to leave the house. This level of instant gratification was unheard of just a few short years ago, but it has quickly become the norm for society. We truly can have what we want and have it now.

These cultural evolutions affect our industry in a fairly profound way. The idea of what timely service means has changed accordingly. Many people have grown far less patient with what they are willing to accept in terms of how long things take from start to finish. This does not mean that we need to rush the process in such a way that will diminish our own standards, but it is something we must be aware of when planning to meet the expectations of our Guests. The thing to remember is that when service lags, it can have a far more negative impact than in years past. People simply have less tolerance for things that take too long.

Perhaps most importantly, when Guests have to wait, they are left to wonder. Let's say Dave is dining at a steakhouse. He is enjoying his cocktail, but the appetizer has taken over twenty minutes now to arrive to the table. His server came by once, about five minutes prior, to let him know that she would check on the food, but she has not returned.

As the minutes go by, Dave begins to wonder. First he wonders what could be going on in the kitchen that is causing the delay. After a few more minutes, he begins to wonder why the server has not returned. One more minute, and he begins to wonder what else is going to go wrong the rest of the evening. Several more minutes, and now he's wondering if the server or anyone else even cares what's going on. Agitation grows as seconds tick by and Dave's experience, which started as excitement, is quickly turning to dread. He is already saying to his company at the table that he does not think he will ever want to return to this place again.

When our Guests are left to wonder, it is usually not a positive thought that will inhabit that space. So when things are going wrong, sometimes the aspect of timely service that means the most is a timely response that communicates what is going on even if it can't be fixed instantly. As long as Guests know what is happening and that we are taking action to ensure their needs are being met, they will feel partnered and taken care of.

We will explore the art of addressing these types of concerns in a later chapter, but for now, consider how your operation deals with timely service. Are there areas that can be improved?

Although this book does not focus much on the tools of technology, this is where I have seen some of my clients use modern systems to make their operations more efficient. One client in particular has a four-hundred-seat, full-service restaurant and brewery that, despite its size, manages to be one of the most efficient establishments I have seen in terms of timely and attentive service.

Each server is equipped with a handheld device on which they place orders tableside. This allows the servers to spend less time huddled in a corner punching orders into a terminal and more time with the Guests. Every food item, including sodas, coffees, cocktails, and food, has a designated runner, so servers spend less time walking up to eighty yards from their section to the bar and back. Again, this creates more time with the Guests and less time running in between. Each Guest receives their initial drink order in two to three minutes or less.

The restaurant also does not accept cash payments. This allows for less opportunity for theft, takes counting banks and drawers in cash off managers' plates, saves time and money that might have been spent on courier services and the like, and is overall a more efficient form of payment. Finally, to contend with such a large space, all managers and hosts wear radios to communicate, improving their ability to solve problems and assist each other quickly. All of these technological innovations and shortcuts help to support a larger goal at my client's restaurant: They allow Team Members to spend more time creating raving fans.

Critical Requirement of Guest Engagement #3: Give More Than They Could Possibly Pay For

When I go shopping, one of the currents of thought constantly running through my head is "am I getting what I'm paying for?" As I scan the shelves, looking for specific products, I am always sizing up the value-to-cost ratio. The idea that I am getting a really good deal is compelling. Whether it be shopping for groceries, clothing, tires for my car, health insurance or a great meal, I always want to know that I am at the very least getting what I'm paying for. In fact, that is just a basic requirement. If I do not feel like I'm getting a good deal, I will likely not return to shop at that store again. There are simply too many other choices out there that make more sense from a value standpoint.

In the restaurant industry, this standard is much higher. Most people do not have the type of expendable income it takes to dine out regularly, even if it is a casual meal. So when they do splurge, especially in fine dining, their expectations when it comes to value are understandably much higher than normal. When Guests spend in this way, remember this is less of a necessary expense and more of an investment. And most people I know like to make returns on their investments.

Once someone sets foot into our establishment, we as owners and managers now own the responsibility for returning more value than was invested on his part. This is what makes the experience that they are investing in one that they will want to return to. If their investment is paying off with high dividends, they will naturally want to reinvest again and again.

Notice that we have established that one only has to enter, or otherwise engage with, our business in order to have invested in us. The very fact that they have shown up is payment enough for us to begin our relationship with them. This is a very important point, one that many will miss. If we feel that someone has to buy something from us in order to treat them as a Guest, then we need to take a good hard look at our core values and reconsider our criteria. By stipulating that this type of transaction must exist for us to engage, we are putting up a barrier and missing a huge opportunity to invite a potentially lucrative and lasting relationship to develop.

When I think about creating an amazing experience for my Guests, I always think of it, once again, in terms of energy. If I can raise the vibration through ambience, impeccable product, engaging service, and the positivity and sincerity I bring to the table, I know that my efforts will eventually translate into prosperity. When we talk about creating top-line sales and revenue, I see that as the product of energy that we create. If I can create an amazing event, bring in great music, great food and atmosphere, and an overall upbeat, positive vibe, people will be drawn to that, and they will naturally and quite willingly spend money.

Once our relationship with a Guest has begun, it is time for us to make it our duty—not just to provide a return on investment, but to provide more value than anyone could possibly pay for. Imagine if we were able to deliver ten times the value that a Guest had paid for. How good would she feel upon leaving? How many friends would she tell about her great fortune to have connected with us? What type of energy could her response create? Imagine how easy it would be to sell our product again and again if everyone felt like they were getting the deal of the century.

I am not suggesting that we need to lower our prices. While that may be appropriate in some cases, and while there is nothing wrong with strategic promotions, some of which we will discuss in later chapters, competing on price alone can sometimes send the wrong message.

Rather than risk devaluing our offerings, we should focus on adding value. If we can still manage to offer that great value at a lower price than our competitors, even better—as long as this is part of a greater strategy to disrupt the market by giving our Guests more value for less investment on their part. But lowering pricing simply as a means to grab more business, without considering the value we add, is a half-baked plan and should be avoided. The fact is that many Guests will happily pay more for an experience so long as that experience makes them feel ten times better for having invested in us.

The Secret Ingredient: Caring

Whether we are talking about Team Member satisfaction or Guest satisfaction, there is one element that serves as a catalyst for achieving the best possible results. This is the secret ingredient that, when added thoughtfully, brings all the other ingredients together to create something amazing. That secret ingredient is *caring*.

The degree to which we truly care is directly related to the degree of value we provide to both Team Members and Guests. I see caring as being a catalyst for all the ingredients that I've outlined above to work.

It may sound trite to use a recipe as an example, but I believe it's a very good way to illustrate what I mean. When baking a cake, it is not enough to simply throw each ingredient into a bowl. That process alone does not produce a cake at all. Yes, those ingredients must be present, but they also must be stirred and folded a certain way. Then they must be put into the proper vessel for baking. The raw ingredients must be placed in an oven at a certain temperature and baked for a certain period of time under certain conditions to get an optimal product. If none of these things are done with care, we run the risk of getting a product that is subpar at best and disastrous at worst.

In business, caring must equal a sincere desire to serve others. Caring adds incredible value. Often this value may be perceived as intangible, but the feelings that people get from a caring interaction absolutely translate into tangible results. How we make people feel will always make the difference in whether they choose to continue a relationship with us at all. The degree to which we make them feel will also determine the degree of their enthusiasm about our relationship.

This works with both positive and negative experiences. If people leave feeling amazing about their interactions with us, they will likely be eager to return and to tell others to do the same. If they leave feeling let down, or worse, offended by those interactions, they will likely do everything they can to warn others not to engage us at all. When we have a sincere desire to serve others, our interactions with each and every Guest will most likely send the message that we care. And that simple, heartfelt gesture can mean everything, not only to those we serve, but also to every aspect of the business itself.

There is no cost to the business in showing a caring attitude. It's free. But the cost of not caring, or simply being perceived as not caring, can be devastating. As business owners and managers, it is difficult for us to imagine being perceived as uncaring. *Of course* we care. We've spent hours, days, *years* working in, and hopefully on, our businesses in the hopes of growing and expanding every aspect. Each and every day, we show up to work with great intentions and hope for continued success. To say that we do not care would be offensive.

But let's always remember that how we engage our Guests will determine how they perceive us and what level of caring they believe we are capable of. In this way, perception is everything, and as much as we care, we have to be very mindful as to *how* we present ourselves, our solutions, our products, and our services to our Guests. Even the best of intentions can become misguided or misinterpreted. Unfortunately, the world does not judge us on our intentions, but our actions. So we must be sure that all of our actions and interactions with those we serve are in line with our highest sense of purpose. Failure to do this effectively can be an incredibly costly disease, and it will ravage a business.

Remember Dave, the Guest who waited for everything and felt the staff did not care? Imagine how different his experience would have been had someone cared enough to go to him, explain what was going on, and offer to diligently work toward making it right. Imagine if they had followed up even after that to ensure that he was not just satisfied, but delighted with his experience. Imagine what just a small amount of communication would've meant to him. Instead of spreading the word that this place was not to be trusted, he could've walked out that evening a raving fan.

The Bottom Line

Let's quickly recap the hallmarks of our unshakable service model. To be truly unshakable, we as leaders will commit to leading with the broom, setting a positive example for our teams through our actions. We will share the love, taking every opportunity to offer feedback, let our Team Members know where they stand, and show them the path to success. We will shatter the glass ceiling, extending opportunity to those who are willing to work to improve. All of these things will contribute to fostering positive emotions that lead to greater Team Member engagement.

When we care about our Team Members, when we show by our actions that we care about our Guests, our Team Members will be more invested in our goals as well. In this way, fostering engaged Team Members will pave the way for the ultimate goal of engaging our Guests. To provide ultimate engagement, we will also have to continuously raise the bar of our own standards, over-delivering on Guests' already high expectations. We will improve our systems to ensure the most timely service possible, and we will provide more value than our Guests could possibly pay for.

When the secret ingredient, caring, is present in every action, it can transform these goals into positive energy and provide an unshakable framework to create an unforgettable experience for those we serve.

Once we have accomplished this, we are ready for the next phase of development: living the mission.

CHAPTER FOUR

LIVING THE MISSION

"A mission statement is not something you write overnight...fundamentally, your mission statement becomes your constitution, the solid expression of your vision and values. It becomes the criterion by which you measure everything else in your life." –Stephen Covey

---

You've put your mission statement up on the wall. You recited it at company meetings. You believe in the idea it represents. But are you executing it daily, in each interaction? Is the mission just an idea, or something that actually produces results?

In my workshops, I often ask for a show of hands on a number of topics, but this one is particularly enlightening. In a room full of owners and managers, I will ask anyone who can honestly recite their company's mission statement and what it means to them to please stand up. I often warn that they will be called upon, so if they are not completely comfortable reciting their statement and what it means to them, they should probably not stand. Occasionally, about half the room will volunteer, but usually it is far less. Of those standing, I will then ask how many can honestly say that, if they were to poll each of their Team Members, all of them would be able to recite the mission statement as well. At this point, almost everyone will sit down.

If anyone is left, I will ask them if their Team Members know what their role is in delivering the mission each and every day. Occasionally, one or two very enthusiastic leaders will explain to the group their process for how they accomplish this. Understandably, they are proud of the fact that they can confidently say that everyone on their team knows the mission and how to achieve it. These leaders are to be applauded, for they have truly embedded the mission into the culture, turning it into a way of being, rather than just words on a wall. Most owners and managers have not been able to achieve this feat; many aren't even aware of its critical importance.

It may seem hard to imagine that every single person on your team would be able to learn and recite your business's mission—or that every single Team Member needs to. The fact is, while it is likely that some Team Members on a given team are very clear about the company's mission and how it is it achieved, it is unlikely that the entire staff fully understands how the mission translates to their daily actions and interactions. There is often a vast gap between knowing something and actually living it. However, imagine for a moment what it could mean for our businesses if everyone not only had the knowledge to recite the inspirational mission, but were actually dedicated to living it. In this case, taking our Team

Members from the point of knowledge to the point of experience is our job as leaders. We must actualize the mission statement.

Before we can empower our teams to live the mission, some of us must do the work of creating a mission statement in the first place. The unfortunate truth is that some businesses do not have a mission statement at all. Perhaps they have an idea, mantra or some other form of motivation. Or perhaps they've overlooked this critical step altogether. If you fall into this category, don't worry—this chapter will be of the most help in your scenario. In the first section I will lay out the elements of a great mission statement centered around your company's values.

The vast majority of businesses *do* have a mission statement that has been clearly written into the business plan. Perhaps it was well thought out to represent the company's values. Perhaps it is hanging on the walls and embedded in their training materials. In this case, business owners may be tempted to think that they have done their job in terms of getting the message across to their teams.

We may think that, because we as the owners and managers know our missions by heart and feel they guide our daily decisions, we have done enough. However, unless our missions are clearly set into the hearts and minds of each of our Team Members and are consistently delivered upon every day, then there is still work to be done. The second part of this chapter will be helpful to those who fall into this category as well. In it, I will discuss practical ways for owners and managers to ensure that staff understand and carry out the mission in a way that is genuine rather than forced.

Until we are truly living the mission, we must press on.

A Purpose-Driven Mission

Many of us see a mission statement as a necessary tool to guide a business and serve as a compass with which to keep it headed in the right direction. And while creating focus and providing direction are worthy attributes, the purpose of the mission can and should be so much more. In fact, while a mission might seem to give our business purpose, I find it helpful to flip this idea and allow the mission to be driven by the purpose. That is to say, our purpose is what fuels the mission. The purpose is the heartbeat that, when aligned with our values, supports and guides us to take the actions that lead to the results we wish to achieve. If we are not careful, however, we can easily steer off course and begin to falter.

Let's put it another way. A mission statement is WHAT we are trying to do. The purpose behind it is WHY we do it. By orienting ourselves first behind the WHY, we have a strong, meaningful motivation to guide and drive the WHAT. One great example of this can be seen through the success of Patagonia, founded by Yvon Choinard, who began making climbing gear for a small group of enthusiasts in Yosemite in the late 1950s. In the early 1970s, the company made a decision to cease selling pitons, the metal spikes hammered into rock by climbers, which were a mainstay in the business at the time. Concerned that these tools damaged the rocks, Choinard developed a new product made from aluminum that could be wedged in and out of rock by hand, rather than hammered and left behind, providing a more environmentally friendly, less invasive way to climb. Choinard made a choice to leave a reliable market due to his values, and it paid off. Not long after Patagonia introduced this new product to the market, the sale of pitons dropped sharply, and aluminum chocks became an industry standard.

The company took another significant risk when they began sourcing organic cotton for their apparel. Though it aligned with Patagonia's values, the change required not only a large capital investment, but it required building a new supply chain and raising the cost of their clothing. In the long run, the investment has paid off, as the Patagonia brand is now known and sought after for both its quality and commitment to environmental causes. If these and many other crucial decisions had been made with only the bottom line in mind, Patagonia would certainly not be what it is today: a two-hundred-million-dollar brand that is widely recognized as a global leader in environmental sustainability. By putting the values and purpose of the company first, Choinard changed the face of an entire industry. When WHY drives the WHAT, it can be incredibly effective!

Anatomy of a Mission

In order to fully understand how we can not only become more familiar with our missions, but really live the truth that they represent, it will be helpful to dive a little deeper. In the upcoming sections, I will go into depth about the functions of a mission statement and what makes one successful.

One main function of a mission is to simplify our ideal workplace culture and values into a deliverable mantra. Just creating a mission statement is not enough. Unless it is incorporated into our teams' daily actions, it is nothing more than a statement. It must be actionable and utilized as a tool for developing behavior. When used actively, the mission will focus energy and attention, spark new ideas, shape company culture and establish consistency. A truly living mission will serve to define the very experiences of our Team Members and Guests. It will provide a voice for our values and ultimately build brand loyalty.

For those who do not have a mission, it is time to develop one. For those who do, it is important to check in with your mission and make sure it is sound. We will begin this process by looking for several key elements that our missions must possess to ensure the most effective results. In order for a mission statement to be the most powerful tool it can be, it must embody our values, center around emotions, cultivate a service mindset, and be implemented to make a positive impact on our Guests.

Effective Missions #1: Core Values

First, an effective mission should be defined by values. Some owners and operators make the mistake of making their mission all about numbers and sales. Let's face it: We are all here to make money. We must always protect the business and ensure a healthy return on investment.

But the mission should never be focused directly on this pursuit. It should always be focused on actualizing the company's values. We should always remember that our net worth equals how many people we serve and how well we serve them. Remember, a healthy bottom line and maximum profitability is a natural byproduct of being of service to others in an impactful way. In order to be impactful, we must become very good at delivering our core values to our Guests with each and every interaction. And there's no better place to start than through our missions.

The mission of Philz Coffee simply reads "Better people's day."

This is a great example of building core values into the heart of a mission. In fact, it is squarely focused on the company's single most important core value. Notice it does not read "to make better coffee." That sounds nice, but certainly falls flat at best. It also does not say, "to better the bottom line." It may seem silly to use such an example—who would state that their mission was to make more money?—yet this is exactly what many businesses are focusing on the most during day-to-day operations. In so doing, we are looking at things through the wrong lens. We should all be asking ourselves: Does our mission truly focus on our core values, or does it fall short? Does it represent what we are all about, or is it generic? Depending on how we honestly answer these questions, it may be time to revisit and make some fundamental changes.

Effective Missions: #2 Emotional Appeal

The next thing we should ask ourselves is whether our mission centers around emotion. People must feel better for having visited and having interacted with us. Our Guests will respond to a positive emotional experience by returning again and again. Similarly, they will respond to a negative emotional experience by finding another place to invest their time, energy and money. This is where centering our mission statement on emotion can be incredibly powerful. If each of our Team Members is highly focused on delivering a positive emotional experience each and every day, the return on that investment will without question mean the difference between success and failure.

The Cohn Restaurant Group in Southern California holds close to thirty restaurants, all with different, unique concepts. They are a family-owned group and are known in the area for their impeccable service, amazing venues, often with sweeping views and unique locations. Their continued success over the years has been based on a simple philosophy which is reflected in their mission:

"Our aim is not simply to please our Guests, but to make them so happy that the last thing they say to themselves as they are leaving is I cannot wait to come back."

This is a mission focused squarely on the emotional experience of the Guest. It is all about making them feel so happy that they cannot wait to come back, even before they leave! Let's imagine if each and every member of a team made it their mission to make *you* feel so happy that you could not wait to come back. If they were to accomplish this, what would it mean to you? How often would you recommend that experience to others? How successful would a business become if this were their standard?

Effective Missions #3: Service First

Being of service must always be the top priority if we are to succeed in creating raving fans. For a mission to mean something, it must be focused on those that we serve and nothing else. A mission that is self-seeking in any way is misguided. By focusing first on monetary gain or matters of technical operations, we are missing the opportunity to engage with our Guests in the most meaningful way.

We also must always remember that Team Members are our best Guests. Team Members who are invested in the business sincerely and wholeheartedly will contribute more, become more productive and will transfer massively positive energy to our Guests, both at work and out in the community. Never underestimate the power of a happy, committed Team Member.

The Nordstrom brand has become synonymous with service-first culture. Their unwavering commitment to customer service is evident from the moment you walk into any Nordstrom's outlet. Everything—from the neatly arranged garments and accessories for sale, to the sounds and smells and lighting of the atmosphere, to the warm, inviting attitudes of sales associates—is geared toward elevating the experience of the Guest. For more than a century, the company has dedicated itself to following the philosophy of founder J. W. Nordstrom:

"To serve customers better, to always be relevant in their lives and to form lifelong relationships."

What a powerful and deeply engaging goal. The mission of the company goes beyond simply being the best in the industry. It seeks to connect with each and every Guest on a deeper level.

And employees of the brand will also most often describe an experience consistent with these values. When I recently spoke with one former Nordstrom's Team Member, he described a very nurturing experience where he felt his input was heard and his values lined up with the company's on a heart level. He was all too happy to pass that experience along when he served Guests in the store each and every day.

Effective Missions #4: Impact

Finally, a mission statement must have a powerful and lasting impact on our Guests. In order to make any kind of difference and to stand out from the hundreds of other competitors out there, what we give simply must be impactful. Why would anyone want to return and spread the good word about what we are doing otherwise? If we have not made some type of positive, lasting impression, we have fallen far, far short of the goal.

It sounds wonderful to say that our mission must have an impact, but how exactly are we to know if this has actually been achieved? I would like you to consider the idea that if we have done a great job ensuring that the first three elements are present in our mission, and that our entire team is taking consistent action towards delivering the message of the mission each day—that is to say, truly living the mission—that mission will in turn have a direct impact on our Guests' experience. I believe that the fourth element of an effective mission can be achieved essentially by taking action and delivering the first three elements consistently.

At least once a year, I treat my family to a weekend at the Ritz-Carlton resort in Laguna Niguel, CA. The resort is a short forty-minute drive from our home in Southern California, in an area that presents the most beautiful sunsets I have had the privilege of witnessing in any part of the world. The beach offers great surfing and pleasant strolls. It is the perfect place for a staycation without the hassle of flights and extensive travel. But, even with all of the convenience and beautiful scenery, the biggest reason we choose to stay at this particular property is due to the impact that the staff has had on us over the years. From the moment we call to make the reservation to the moment we leave the property, we are made to feel like rockstars. Every person involved, from the bellman to the porter to housekeeping, greets us with a warm smile, and they are always at the ready to assist with anything that we may need.

When you take a look at the Ritz-Carlton's mission, the impact my family has felt is clearly related.

The Ritz-Carlton is a place where the genuine care and comfort of our Guests is our highest mission. We pledge to provide the finest personal service and facilities for our guests who will always enjoy a warm, relaxed, yet refined ambience. The Ritz-Carlton experience enlivens the senses, instills well-being, and fulfills even the unexpressed wishes and needs of our guests.

Notice that this mission expresses core values of sincerity, integrity and genuine hospitality. It is centered around the emotions of well-being and comfort, and it undoubtedly places service above all else. Yet without the actions taken by each and every Team Member to deliver on these words, there would be no impact at all. It is the action of the staff that translates the ideas of the mission into a Guest experience. And this is done through the application of the service values each Team Member should be trained to consistently deliver. Here are some of those service values from the Ritz-Carlton, each of which deliver on the promise of the mission.

I build strong relationships and create Ritz-Carlton guests for life.

I am always responsive to the expressed and unexpressed wishes and needs of our Guests.

I am empowered to create unique, memorable and personal experiences for our Guests.

I continuously seek opportunities to innovate and improve The Ritz-Carlton experience.

I own and immediately resolve Guest problems.

I am proud of my professional appearance, language and behavior.

This is where the real impact occurs. These are the actions that lead to the experience my family and I receive each time we visit. This is what keeps us coming back again and again. This is how the Ritz-Carlton team is living their mission.

Going Off Book

Having spent many years as a professional actor, I understand that one of the goals in the process of developing a character is learning to take the words from the page and give them life. Actors are not tasked with simply memorizing lines, but taking their lines and turning them into a very real emotional experience through behavior, speech and performance. Part of this process is referred to as "going off book." When an actor is able to put the script down and allow the character to actually inhabit their space, the transformation from written word to experience has begun.

Imagine a play in which all the actors are simply reading their lines from a script, with no real feelings, engagement, or chemistry. It is unlikely that an audience would sit through the entire two-hour play. It is when the players seem to be living the scene through their own experience that the show becomes interesting, and, when done well, even inspiring and soul-stirring.

Just like the team at the Ritz-Carlton, the goal for every team should be to take the company mission from the written statement on the page to a place of actual experience. Once everyone, from the upper management to the dishwashers, understands the mission on an experiential level, they can begin to deliver it effectively.

We may be aware of the impact of a mission statement, and we may have crafted our mission with all the elements needed for it to be a powerful tool, but unless it is put into practice every day, the mission will never go off book.

The actor rehearses her lines over and over while exploring different aspects of the character. With each rehearsal, she grows more comfortable with the role, so that once the production is launched, she is free to fully express the character. That is when the magic happens. When the role is played well, the energy between the actor and the audience can be electrifying.

No, I am not suggesting that we make our teams memorize and repeat the mission statement ad nauseum. The point is to allow the mission to become a way of being. The "rehearsal" of the mission is not just memorizing the lines, but the day-to-day practice, incorporating the spirit of what the mission represents into everything that we do.

When the members of our teams are comfortable in their roles, when they are expressing the mission as intently as the actor would the intention of a character, a similar magic suffuses their performance. When a server steps out onto the floor, he is on stage. His Guests are his audience. The food runners and server assistants play supporting roles. The general manager directs. The hosts welcome Guests into the theater. The chef and kitchen teams are master stagehands and set designers. We are not in the business of serving food. We are in the business of entertaining, and food is the extra dimension, our competitive advantage.

The mission statement of the business serves a role similar to what actors would call the subtext of a script. It is the heartbeat, the essence, the main intention of the message. And as owners and managers, each and every shift, it is our responsibility to direct our teams toward the performance of the century. We set the stage, dim the lights, and the curtains go up. Guests are ushered into the theatre and we entertain, hoping to leave them spellbound, captivated and wanting more.

At Everbowl, one of the fastest-growing quick-service concepts in Southern California, craft superfood is not the only thing on the menu. Not only do they have the tastiest bowls of healthy food, they have the warmest, friendliest staff around. When you walk into any Everbowl location, you are instantly greeted with a huge smile and a warm "welcome to Everbowl!" The vibe is upbeat, bright, clean, and inviting. At Everbowl, the staff understands that they are not in the restaurant business, but the entertainment business. They just also happen to serve amazing food that is colorful, healthy, fresh and fun. The mission of this fast-growing concept is preached daily and directly relatable to its incredible success. "Make friends and have fun" is not only a written statement, it is truly lived by each and every one of its staff members.

When taken to heart, a mission such is this has a massive impact, not only on the community but on the Team Members as well. The leadership of Everbowl has done an incredible job of building everything around this mission. If you walk into an Everbowl location and ask any of its young staff members what their mission is, they will happily recite "make friends and have fun!" For many of their Team Members, this statement in and of itself is an exciting concept. It is a role that is fun to play and brings joy to their lives. And that spirit of joy gets passed on to every Guest that walks in. Bright smiles and welcoming attitudes are the norm at Everbowl, making it somewhere people just want to be.

From Concept to Reality

Now that we have strengthened our resolve to do everything we can to take our mission from the written page to the Guest experience, it is time to ensure that our entire team is armed with the tools they need to implement and live the mission themselves. There are several things we can implement to ensure the mission is well integrated into the culture and turns from a vague concept or idea into a daily practice; turning it into "just how we do things."

At first glance, we may feel we are already doing everything we can in this regard. We may look across the scope of our teams and feel that we have a strong culture oriented around our mission. But we must challenge ourselves to be honest here. We must ask ourselves if we could have done better yesterday and if we can do better today.

Were there any opportunities where we could have done more to "better peoples' day"? Could we have worked harder to "make them so happy…they could not wait to come back"? Did we "have fun and make friends with everyone"? If we are truly honest with ourselves, we will find that there is always room for improvement. We as leaders must become obsessed with living the mission and therefore providing ourselves as an example. We must recommit daily. We must always keep ourselves in check and be honest as to how well we are achieving this goal. This is the first step toward ensuring that living the mission becomes an integral part of our workplace culture.

In my restaurants, I expect that all leaders on the team are taking this seriously by making it part of how they are evaluated. Everyone understands the importance of holding themselves to this standard, as I always ask, "What have we done today to fulfill our mission?" Stay committed and expect your teams to show the same commitment.

In this section, I'll bring in some practical, everyday commitments we can make to ensure success, including prominent messaging, sharing and celebrating examples of great service, and practicing mission-driven hiring practices.

From Concept to Reality Commitment #1: Share the Message

With our newfound strength and resolve to live the mission, we must begin sharing the message with our teams in every way possible. We can start by posting the message in pertinent and high-visibility areas for our teams to see. I always have a printed version of our mission framed and hung in our kitchen where it can be easily seen by all Team Members. It is prominent and presented artfully so as to give it an air of importance. This is one way our teams know that it is important to us, and that it must be important to them.

Another must-do is posting the mission at the top of every training guide for new Team Members. We must make it prominent and repetitive. Team Members that are just entering our culture should be exposed to the mission as much as possible so they can easily remember it and understand the importance of incorporating this philosophy into their work from the very beginning. The sooner they get on board, the better.

Another step is set the tone for team meetings with the mission, using it as a guide for every decision that is made. I usually begin each meeting with the recital of the mission as a reminder, keeping it at the top of every agenda.

When we refer to it often, the mission will become the paradigm for all discussions, and will keep things moving in the right direction.

From Concept to Reality Commitment #2: Share Examples

By sharing examples of how to live the mission with our teams daily, we can effectively inspire our teams to align their actions with the idea—as well as encouraging them to share examples themselves. As Team Members go about their days with the mission at the top of their minds, they will naturally find ways to accomplish our goals more effectively.

Remember, the mood that we pass along to others is usually dictated by whatever our state of being happens to be at the time. A crappy mood equals crappy service. When we have a mission oriented around a positive emotion, living it by example helps to set the tone for a shift to a better emotional state.

Suppose I ask Christine, the lead host, what challenges she faced this week when dealing with any upset Guests. She will likely be able to remember at least one encounter that was difficult for her. Perhaps it was Joe, a regular who was upset that his table was not ready when he arrived. If I ask Christine how she handled this, she may say something like, "I let Joe know that we had a Guest that was enjoying their experience a little longer than we anticipated, and that I would get him settled as soon as possible, or else I could offer him another table right away. I also offered to get Joe a drink at the bar while he was waiting if he would like."

With an example like this, I would praise Christine for living our mission. Clearly she did everything she could to make this Guest super happy.

On the other hand, if her response was, "well, I told Joe I was sorry, I'd get him settled as quickly as I could," and the story ended there, I might coach Christine on how to go further to ensure that Joe was super happy, rather than leaving his experience to chance and risk having him become more upset if we were not able to accommodate quickly.

Can you see the difference here in the two examples? By sharing our stories and examples with each other, we create daily coaching opportunities and ways to really teach our teams how to go the extra mile to live the mission. When we skip out on sharing, we are missing some golden opportunities.

From Concept to Reality Commitment #3: Celebrate the Wins

I love a practice that one of my favorite restaurants has established to celebrate when a Team Member really lives the mission. Each time someone on the team does something outstanding that truly embodies their mission, they are given a little gift, and openly celebrated. In this case, the Team Member receives "restaurant bucks," a coupon for a designated amount that can be spent like cash at the restaurant, whether it's put toward Team Member meals or when dining off the clock. Some Team Members will save these up for a special occasion or to treat their family or friends when they visit. When they are gifted the coupon, management makes it a big deal with high-fives and excitement, and those who consistently receiving lots of the coupons are also recognized in all-staff or department meetings and in the company newsletter.

These celebrations are not only encouraging for those who receive recognition, but they're also motivating to everyone who witnesses the celebration. Openly celebrating their achievements with Team Members reinforces their commitment to living the mission and fosters an overall positive work environment.

From Concept to Reality Commitment #4: Hire Only Mission-Driven People

In order to cultivate a team of rockstar brand ambassadors, it's a good idea to be thinking of the mission from the very beginning. We must hire and retain only those who are fully committed to living the mission. Asking questions related to a candidate's philosophy around Guest service and how he would approach certain situations is top priority.

When I am interviewing a candidate, I tend to spend less time on questions regarding their technical ability and far more time trying to understand their personal philosophy on Guest service. I want to know how they have reacted in situations when things became difficult. I try to understand the energy they bring to their work by asking them to describe in detail how they deliver an amazing experience. I ask for examples of what their former coworkers and employers would say about them if asked about their personal experience.

If I do not leave the interview feeling excited to work with this person and even inspired by their genuine desire to be of service to others, then that candidate is a no-go. If we are going to bring someone onto our team, that person must be able to demonstrate that they will sincerely and wholeheartedly devote themselves to the mission at hand. They must convince us that they are not just here to come along for the ride, but to lead the charge.

By the same token, if a once-great Team Member seems to have lost the spark, we must also address this immediately. We as leaders need to identify when someone has strayed from the path and quickly redirect them back in alignment with the mission. Everyone must be in coordinated lockstep and moving in the same direction together with vigor. Our train is heading north, and we are either on it together, or it is time to get off at the next stop.

The Bottom Line

Spending time on developing and delivering our companies' mission is crucial to our long-term success. Too often, the daily grind takes over and these necessary steps and commitments are overlooked, leaving little room for our true mission to shine through. Now that we are aware of the elements of a successful mission statement and have some examples of how to put it into action, we have all the building blocks we need to utilize this powerful tool.

By fully exploring the elements that make a mission work, we can create a statement that centers on company values and human experience. And by teaching everyone on our team how to express the mission in every interaction, we can unleash a powerful inner resource that will transform how we do business, what our Team Members feel about working for us, how we are seen in the marketplace, and how our Guests feel when they step into our establishments. This is the type of energy that both Team Members and Guests will be thrilled to be a part of, and *that* is a recipe for lasting success.

CHAPTER FIVE

A PROGRAM OF ATTRACTION

"Coming together is a beginning. Keeping together is progress. Working together is success." – Henry Ford

---

Once I had a restaurant owner call me for advice regarding how much to spend on ads in social media. He had been placing ads on Facebook, Instagram and Yelp and was trying to determine the right mix for his business. He shared that he had recently increased his spend on Yelp alone to just over $5,000 per month. With annual gross revenues of just under two million dollars per year, he was spending over five percent of his total gross sales on advertising alone, almost exclusively on social media and print ads.

If you've paid attention to the last four chapters, you may be guessing that I had some suggestions for this business owner. And you'd be right.

As I told this client, the major problem with the strategy of pumping money into online media is that it can be very difficult to measure a true Return On Investment (ROI) for restaurants in these mediums. Let's take Yelp, for example. While it is true that Yelp does a good job of ranking businesses within their own platform, and it is a very well-known source for finding businesses like restaurants in a specific area, it is still very difficult to know which Guests came through the door specifically because they found us on Yelp.

Similarly, while print advertising may make sense in some circumstances, especially highly targeted ads with verifiable outcomes, such as a coupon or special promotion, these types of ads can grow to be quite costly. Simply placing an ad about our restaurant in a magazine, for instance, may be a very costly way to reach our audience with no real sense of a true ROI. Unless we are a major corporation with a very large marketing and advertising budget—and even then—we may want to be cautious about making sure every dollar we spend has a maximum return on investment.

This is not to say we should not advertise on Yelp or other similar sites. There are ways to take advantage of our presence on Yelp, some of which we will discuss in the final chapter. However, we should be very careful as to how much we are willing to invest in this type of advertising. At some point, the rate of return begins to diminish, and we have very little control over the outcome in many of these scenarios.

This is not the only drawback of focusing all of our promotional energy and money on outside strategies. It can also take the place of more important developments inside the business. As I discussed in Chapter Two, for our businesses to naturally draw Guests in and keep them coming back for more, for any advertising we do on outside platforms to be worthwhile, we first must have a solid foundation within our four walls. As I pointed out in Chapter Two, part of this foundation is making sure that everything is working fine under the hood, that we have systems in place to handle the daily grind and allow us as owners and managers to work on our businesses rather than in them.

And part of this foundation is, before looking to outside advertising, learning to utilize the resources that we already have at our disposal—our location, our personal connections, our unique spaces and ways to create extra value, our day-to-day practice of our mission, our Team Members' expertise and enthusiasm—to turn Guests themselves into ambassadors promoting our brand.

The Courtship

We must promote our businesses. We may have the best pancakes in town, but people must come to try them, or we will never reap the benefit of that fact. Our happy hour may be the best value around, but without a volume of people coming to enjoy what we are offering, our seats will remain empty. We have worked hard to create something that we believe others will want. Yet, unless we can get butts in seats, the pain of defeat will quickly overwhelm us.

When faced with this great challenge, many business owners will want to jump to technology as a means to get quick business coming into the building. In some cases, this may be the right thing to do. Perhaps running a Groupon ad for several months will introduce enough new people in order to get things going. Placing Yelp, Google and Facebook ads may be the best option to target our geographic area and raise awareness about our brand. These types of advertising can be very effective when done right and within the budget designated for marketing.

Engaging with and even advertising on social media can make very good sense, but simply throwing dollars into those platforms without any consideration for how we are actually interacting with our demographic is foolish. By understanding who we serve and how we can best serve them, we can make informed decisions on how to most effectively reach them.

There are many experts out there who can give great advice on how to manage and engage on social media. I will not be focusing on this aspect. Instead, we will look closer to home.

If we are to create lasting, meaningful relationships with our Guests, we will need to build a marketing platform that is based on attraction—drawing people in and keeping them excited once they are here—rather than promotion alone. After all, we are courting our Guests, and, like any courtship, we will want to create value that our potential partners, our Guests, will want to invest in and to be a part of. A great program of attraction will ensure that those we serve feel that they are better off for having experienced what we have offered.

In this chapter, we will dive deeply into creating our own unique program of attraction that is organic, authentic, and specifically designed to offer great experiences that will keep Guests engaged and informed about what we do and how we do it. In later sections, we will discuss multiple promotional strategies, both inside and outside the business, that are often overlooked in favor of big spending on social media. We will also spend some time on how to optimize our outside promotions and make sure we are getting a return on our investment. However, let us begin by exploring what a program of attraction looks like, including the key values that our promotions need to have to organically keep Guests returning again and again.

Elements of Attraction #1: In the Driver's Seat

In my restaurants, I always pay close attention to whether the promotion that we are offering is something that Guests are simply stumbling upon, or if the promotion itself is driving sales. Are people simply taking advantage of it because it is there, or does it actually drive business?

I once had a manager who suggested that we should promote an aggressive Wine Wednesday program in which we would offer the entire wine list at fifty percent off each Wednesday. Reluctantly, I gave it a shot, and paid close attention to see if we could increase our cover counts as a result.

For about six months, we ran the program, and, while wine sales certainly increased, our cover counts did not. It seemed that no more people were actually coming through our door than before. Instead, more Guests were taking advantage of the deep discount. In this scenario, we ended up losing money. Yes, my wine sales increased, but my promotional expense line did as well, with no real bump in business to speak of. This is what we would call a "stumble-upon" promotion.

With this awareness, we then decided to create a Wine Wednesday list that was made of select bottles instead. We offered a nice selection with varied price ranges, but focused on only certain bottles to ensure we were selling those that we had gotten a good deal on, had extras of in the inventory, or otherwise wanted to move out. As an added measure, we added a hand-picked selection called Ryan's list, named for the wine director at the time. This added a personal touch, and many Guests would ask to meet Ryan when shopping for wine. In addition, we scheduled Ryan to always work on Wednesdays, when he would visit each table to talk about wines, make suggestions and up-sell the experience.

As people got to know Ryan and receive a very personalized experience, our sales on Wednesdays began to grow; we received more Guests into the dining room, and the check averages climbed as well. While taking the Guest experience to another level, this promotion became a real driver of sales and covers. This should always be the goal of a good promotion.

Elements of Attraction #2: All About the Experience

One powerful way to ensure our promotions have the best chance at driving sales is to focus on experiences. While there is nothing inherently wrong with giving a simple discount or running a sale-based promotion, it helps to come up with promotions that offer a great experience that our Guests can get nowhere else. This can be an incredibly powerful way to differentiate us from our competitors and drive business.

At a funky little bistro in Norfolk, Virginia, Tuesday nights are considered "date night." The popular downtown hotspot offers

Nuevo Latino cuisine and craft cocktails in a chic setting. Two people can receive two entrees and a bottle of wine or carafe of sangria for a mere $39.95.

The great part about this promotion is not just the attractive price point, although that certainly is quite notable. What really drives this is the idea behind it. Not only does it position the restaurant as the perfect place to bring a date with little upfront investment, it entices friends to get together to take advantage of the deal as well. It effectively positions an experience in the minds and hearts of visiting Guests before they even arrive. "Date Night" sounds fun and inviting; the name itself paints an enticing picture of the type of experience one might receive when coming to enjoy the promotion.

And it is proving to be quite effective. Before offering the promotion, the restaurant's cover counts on a typical Tuesday night averaged around fifty to seventy people. Since beginning the promotion two years ago, they have consistently received over *two hundred* Guests each Tuesday night, and it does not seem to be slowing. The spot has become known as a place to bring your date (or good friends) for a great deal. As for the $39.95 price point, well, Guests are also given the option to upgrade their entrées and wine selection for an additional cost, allowing an opportunity for increased revenue, as well as a higher-level experience, if the Guest should choose it: a win-win for everyone.

This type of offering goes beyond simply promoting the business. It works toward making the brand synonymous with a fun, cool experience. Perhaps this is why I have implemented this same type of program, with other restaurants in different markets, and seen similar success.

Elements of Attraction #3: Driving Value

People tend to spend based on the value they perceive they will receive. When we as owners and managers begin to see our offerings in terms of their value to the Guest, we are better able to entice our Guests to invest more with us. Increasing sales often comes by increasing the value we add to each experience.

In Oceanside, CA, the sun sets on the dining room of a hip, upscale eatery overlooking the pier, where the smell of ocean air accents the masterfully prepared seafood and steak offerings that the chef has created. The restaurant is also a local favorite, boasting not only world-class cuisine, but an incredibly approachable happy hour with over one hundred vodkas from around the world and delightful bites at a much lower price than you might expect in a restaurant of this caliber.

 While many might think that this offering alone could be enough to drive business and sales, it is the experience itself that ensures locals and tourists alike will keep coming back. Not only is the staff friendly, the bartenders are always eager to draw you in and craft something special for you, offer a vodka tasting, or otherwise educate on the finer points of wine and spirits production. Everyone on staff takes pride in their work, their knowledge of food and drink and their ability to create relationships. The general manager is always there to greet Guests as they arrive, and she and her management team spend all of their time during service walking from table to table, ensuring each Guest has a personal, warm experience.

Whether you are celebrating, seriously dining, or just stopping in for a cheap cocktail, as a Guest, everyone you encounter during your stay makes you feel like a part of the family. Not only do you feel you have received an incredible amount of value from the experience, but you feel valued as a person. Very impactful.

Providing a little something extra, breaking the rules and being serious about hospitality will turn any promotion into something much more. It is simply not enough to tell people that we have a great happy hour. We must give something of far more value in order to make it effective. Giving our Guests what they paid for is fine, but providing more value than they could ever have possibly paid for is truly winning. This is the kind of experience that Guests will return for again and again.

This is what the mental shift from driving sales to driving value looks like. If we focus on the value that we add, both when creating our promotions and in everything that we do, we will attract more and more Guests by virtue of synergy. The energy of hospitality builds upon itself and becomes something people simply want to be a part of. This is why driving value must be our number one focus.

Reaching Out

Contrary to popular belief, if you build it, they may not come. Alas, simply because we have the best location, the best menu, and a great sign out front does not mean Guests will come pouring into our place. This is the point of promotions: Sometimes we have to reach out to untapped markets to let them know who we are, what we offer, and why we are the best choice for them.

Now that we learned the most essential elements that a successful promotion needs to take advantage—the resources already inside our businesses—it's time for some practical solutions. These promotional opportunities, which are by no means an exhaustive list, range from old-fashioned to newfangled, but I find they are often underutilized by most business owners. Keeping the elements of attraction in mind, we can begin to understand the resources that we have within our businesses and communities, and open up whole new areas of influence.

Overlooked Promotional Opportunities #1: The Ask

Sometimes the best way to promote our brand and to get our Guests to return is to simply invite them to do so.

Beverly is a server that is passionate about service. She takes great pride in not only giving a great Guest experience, but also in being the most-requested server on staff. Her name regularly appears in five-star Yelp reviews, and rarely will she work a shift without a specific request for her to serve a table.

This does not happen by accident. When I asked Beverly how she accomplishes this, she replied, "I just ask."

"Okay, can you be more specific?"

"Sure. I start by asking how their day is going. Getting to know quickly where they are at allows me to understand how I can best be of service to them. I ask them questions about their preferences of food and wine so I can guide them through what might be best for their dining experience. I ask if there are any details that I may provide that can make their experience better. As things are coming to an end, I ask them how my service has been and if they have enjoyed everything while they were here. And finally, I ask them to leave a review for the restaurant and to request me on their next visit. Asking questions means that I am listening, and that creates a bond between me and my Guests."

Well, I am certainly glad I asked. What a simple yet effective way to make friends with those we serve, and to ensure they leave wanting to come back again. Imagine if every single person on staff used this technique to engage with Guests. This type of promotion is highly targeted and costs zero marketing dollars to implement. It only requires hiring people like Beverly, who really care, and training our teams to emulate her behavior.

Overlooked Promotional Opportunities #2: Neighbors to Neighbors

We have all seen the guy flipping the sign on the corner to draw drivers-by in for the special of the week. We have also received the flyer on our windshield advertising a great deal for the business down the street. These are good ideas, and, if done properly, can be effective at times. But reaching out can also include a more personal touch that I have found to produce verifiable results.

A dear friend of mine is an event planner. She had a position at an event facility that housed a restaurant as well as several meeting rooms and a beautiful outdoor patio with fire features, cabanas, and a bar. It truly was a unique space, and so inviting that it almost seemed to sell itself. Despite this, she was having difficulty meeting her goals in filling the space with enough business. After discussing the issue and brainstorming possible solutions, we came up with a sketch of a marketing plan that included several potential markets that might be interested in the space.

One of her premiere spaces was a room that could accommodate up to fifty Guests for dinner. The room was in close proximity to the kitchen for easy execution, and the decor matched the modern rustic feel of the restaurant itself. Most of the time, the space was used for overflow dining on busy nights or for private social gatherings. From time to time, the room would also be rented by pharmaceutical companies and local financial planners to give presentations to potential clients. We decided that those markets should be explored further, and came up with a goal of increasing that business from an average of one day per week to an average of three days per week.

We made a list of all of the financial planners within a ten-mile radius, put together a simple marketing piece that introduced the space to them as a potential for their future presentations, and reached out to invite them down to tour the space. We heard from one of our best pharmaceutical clients that their industry was holding a meeting for all of the reps in the area to get together and discuss new products and industry best practices. We arranged to have one of these groups meet at my friend's location and provided light hors d'oeuvres for the group as an enticement. Within several months, both of these markets began to hold more and more events there, and our goal of three events per week was met, and in some weeks, surpassed.

Going through the brainstorming process, we also recognized another untapped market that seemed a little more out of left field, but completely viable. The week before our meeting, a family held a celebration of life at my friend's venue and had commented that it was so heartwarming to know that they did not have to worry about that detail while they were grieving their loss. We decided to reach out to all of the mortuaries in the area to let them know that her space was available to host celebrations of life. The marketing took into account the idea that her business would be there during a troubling time to handle all of the details necessary to make the celebration something memorable and delivered with love. Within the month, several celebrations of life booked the space.

My friend now has relationships set up with key partners in the community that recommend her business when there is a true need, and it is known that she will be there to take care of every detail, thereby making the decision of where to host an event very easy one to make.

With some degree of creativity, and with a willingness to reach out, we can drive business while providing a real solution to those we serve.

Overlooked Promotional Opportunities #3: Bouncing Back

As I've discussed before, getting people to come to the party first requires that we simply invite them. We can do this by promoting on social media, through our email list, or in various forms of advertisement and signage. But one tool that is often overlooked is marketing directly to those who are already in the building.

Let's say that we are holding an event of some kind in which a hundred attendees have come to participate. It is very likely that many of these people have never been to our business before. Not only is it imperative that we do our best to impress these Guests while they are with us, it is also a great opportunity to provide them with a "bounce back" promotion in the form of an invite to return at a later date. In many cases, this invite includes a discount on food, a free appetizer, or some type of gift for returning.

In retail, it is not uncommon to be given a "ten percent off your next purchase" coupon upon checkout. This is nice, but given that I shop the clearance racks anyway, I'm often not likely to be highly motivated to return for this. It just seems lackluster. But one restaurant took the concept of a bounce back and added a compelling twist.

During the month of December, each table received a small wrapped gift, each containing an offering to be redeemed in January, which is traditionally a slower month in restaurants. The gift contained anything from a free dessert, to free valet parking for a year, to a private beer dinner for four. The catch was that the gift was not to be opened until they returned in January.

Some friends and I accumulated several of these gifts and returned in January to see what we had won. While we did not win big, the restaurant sure did. When we really focus on adding value, when we truly go beyond the typical promotion that our Guests are used to, we can create very unique and effective promotions that really set us apart.

Another great example of a bounce back program that really worked is one that I learned about from a friend who was a successful concert promoter. Despite the fact that she had a huge following from all of the events she promoted over the years, she never rested on her laurels. At each show, she would spend time mingling among the crowd, getting to know the attendees. When she made a connection, she would always ask people's music preferences and inquire if they were interested in artists that she knew had upcoming shows. Once she discovered a fan of someone she happened to be promoting in the near future, she would give them a special voucher to bring to the show with them.

This was not a free ticket. On the contrary, they would have to pay for their ticket as everyone else would. Each voucher was a specific color, which would match a particular giveaway for that evening. Depending on which evening it was, the Guest could redeem their voucher for a prize that matched that color. One night, blue might be a free beverage at the bar, green might be VIP access or front-row seating, and red might be a backstage pass.

The Guests would not know which level of prize they could claim until they arrived at the show, but regardless, everyone was a winner. My friend could easily track the amount of vouchers that were returned for any given show to see how her promotion was going. This was just one of many win-win promotional tactics that she used over the years to build a strong and loyal following for her and her venues.

Overlooked Promotional Opportunities #4: Growing the Tribe

While I've discussed several tips for innovative and creative tricks to get people in the door, the best, most cost-effective way to market to those we serve still remains the email list. Regardless of our reach on social media, an email list allows us to broadcast targeted, personalized promotions to those who are, based on their opt-in, already completely open to receiving the information.

While we should always take full advantage of whichever social media platform is best suited for our demographic, an email list must be an integral part of our marketing program. We should be constantly inviting Guests to provide their email address to us in an effort to build a base of leads with which we can share information on upcoming events, recipes, special promotions, and insider deals. With a solid base audience to market to, we can self-produce monthly events that are guaranteed to sell out.

I should note that, depending on your demographic, you may opt for text or app marketing as a means to grow a following. I suggest doing your research on which technology is best for your tribe and taking into consideration that some platforms may become less relevant over time. So far, email remains a constant, reliable form of data collection and delivery.

One of my favorite breweries regularly holds beer dinners and beer-tasting events with different themes throughout the year. In speaking with the general manager, I asked how he promotes them and seems to sell out every single time. He told me that in two short years, he has been able to grow his marketing list to just over twelve *thousand* contacts and uses this list exclusively to sell and promote his events.

At every event, and in his tasting room and restaurant, he offers a $7 coupon—the exact cost of a craft beer—in exchange for a Guest's email address and birthday. The coupon is delivered through the email that the Guest signs up with to ensure it is a valid email address. Meanwhile, the birthday is kept on file, to be acknowledged each year with a birthday gift, separate from the $7 coupon, sent to the recipient.

The entire staff is trained to offer this to each new Guest they meet, and he sometimes runs a staff contest with prizes for the winner who attains the most email addresses for the month. He not only continues to build his list, but the email itself serves as a bounce back, and people come to his brewery to celebrate their birthdays constantly throughout the year. A free beer in exchange for an email address? That's a no-brainer. And it is highly effective.

Overlooked Promotional Opportunities #5: Common Ground

Groups that conduct any type of business need spaces to meet. In the modern economy, more and more businesses conduct meetings outside of a traditional office setting. Coffee shops are littered with young professionals tapping on laptop keyboards while sipping their favorite cold brew. Hundreds of professional industries use restaurants to hold dinners and events for recruiting purposes, whether it be new Team Members or new clients. Lively spaces with food, decor and atmosphere often win the day over stark offices as meeting places.

Yet, surprisingly, many restaurants fail to see their space as a place for groups like these to congregate. I once hosted a meetup group at our restaurant for single parents. The host of the group commented to me about how happy they were that it was so easy for them to arrange being there. Happy to hear this, I inquired further to get details of what he meant. He explained that most places he called to host his modest group of twenty to thirty single parents seem as if they don't want them there. He went on to say that it is not uncommon to feel as if their group is more of an imposition than a wanted Guest.

"I know that sometimes people hear 'meetup' and they just assume that we will not spend enough money to warrant the work it takes to host us, and perhaps in some cases that can be true, but I am surprised when I walk into their establishment at 7 PM on a Saturday night and they have very little business going on to begin with. You would think a group like ours would bring much-needed energy to the place."

I thanked him for his perspective and thought about this for a bit.

Once again, I firmly believe that money is a form of energy. The exchange that happens when money is flowing is a more excited form of that energy. Before we can get to that point, however, we must create the conditions that produce energy and will ultimately lead to that exchange. People getting together and sharing experiences, with great food, music, ambience, and positive energy, creates heightened emotion. It is in this emotional state the people are most likely to exchange more energy, including money.

By making our space one that people feel welcome to congregate in and inviting them to do so on a regular basis, we are able to create the type of energy that leads to a great experience for everyone present. It is through the culmination of these experiences that we are able to benefit from the sales that occur along the way. It is baffling to me how many businesses spend so much time, money and effort to build the perfect space, create the perfect menu and train and hire the right people—only to miss the opportunity to create the energy it takes to be successful.

By making our space a common ground to be shared by all, we can take full advantage of this opportunity. Business leaders, entrepreneurs, groups and organizations of all kinds, love to meet at restaurants. As owners and managers, we should be constantly involving ourselves in the process of connecting with these groups and inviting them to come and share our space in fun and creative ways. From business meetings to group meetups to paint nights to medical presentations, making our space desirable to these groups will ultimately be profitable, and will certainly introduce Guests to our establishment who might not have otherwise given us a shot.

Overlooked Promotional Opportunities #6: The Power of Partnerships

One more often-overlooked, yet incredibly effective promotional strategy can be found in partnerships. Teaming up with local chambers of commerce, community organizations, neighboring businesses, schools, or nonprofits can drive benefits to both parties when explored creatively. A central goal of all of these entities is to raise awareness and increase the effectiveness of their respective organizations. By finding ways to help each other accomplish this, through alignment and by leveraging one another's customer or member base, we can create a win-win situation for all involved.

One of my clients has a restaurant near an area populated by various car dealerships. It is a unique casual fine dining space with a locally renowned chef, some meeting rooms, and a modern rustic dining room. His clientele is similar to that of several of the dealerships nearby, catering to folks with a modest income; those who have a champagne taste, yet still appreciate a good deal. He began building relationships with the dealerships nearby, running special pricing on certain items for dealership Team Members, as well as creating some car-themed cocktails that the salespeople could enjoy after work. He created a nice little business for himself by making his spot a go-to place for those who worked at the dealerships, their friends, and their families.

One afternoon, while having a conversation with one of the top sales managers at the Lexus dealership, he learned that Lexus was looking for a way to add value to their customer experience. The owner of the dealership was very interested in creating more of a lifestyle-brand identity and thought that hospitality was a key element to this. My client asked to be introduced to the owner to discuss how they might be able to come together to benefit each other along the lines of this type of experience.

The following week, he met with the owner of the dealership and proposed that, if she would be interested in purchasing gift certificates to the restaurant for anyone who had purchased a car, he would sell them to her at a discount. She agreed that this would be a great program and purchased multiple $100 gift cards for $75 each.

But rather than simply give the gift card away to the new Lexus owner, it was important to both parties that they gave their client the full experience. They both knew that it would be much more valuable to make the experience a much bigger deal than simply giving someone a coupon or gift card that might or might not ever be used. To solve this problem, the partners came up with a program that would ensure an elevated experience. Whenever a new car was sold, the salesperson would call to make a reservation to the restaurant on behalf of the client. The restaurant would mark the reservation as a new Lexus owner, indicating that when the Guest came to dine, they would receive special treatment that was aligned with the Lexus brand.

Each of these Guests would be greeted by the manager and welcomed on behalf of the restaurant as well as the Lexus dealership. The server would know the name of the salesperson, as indicated in their notes on the Guest from the call, and would use this as a point of familiarity to make them feel comfortable. The chef would send a small amuse-bouche to open the experience and finish with a small dessert marked with a Lexus logo made of chocolate.

In this scenario, each Guest would be made to feel like royalty simply because they had been sent by the restaurant's Lexus preferred partner. With an average of over two hundred cars sold by the dealership per month, this resulted in a value of at least

$15,000 in extra revenue for the restaurant per month—not even including additional purchases and repeat business. It also aligned the two brands in the community and created a buzzworthy energy that continued to build upon itself.

Upselling Ourselves

When most of us think of promotion, we think in terms of promoting our brand. This is logical, since promotions are meant to build sales through increasing awareness. By exposing our brand to more people in meaningful ways, we increase our chances of converting them into paying customers.

If we are to take this concept and apply it not only to our brand itself, but to the experience we give, we have the opportunity to share what we do and how we do it on a much deeper level. When Guests are dining in our restaurants, they have already qualified as those who could become ambassadors of our brand. They are immersed in the atmosphere we have created. They appear to be enjoying the product we serve and they are experiencing the service we provide. If all is going according to plan, they are being lavished in hospitality and they are feeling quite good. This is the perfect time to promote a potentially greater experience.

We have all heard of upselling. In restaurants, this is when a server might suggest adding a lobster tail to a steak dinner as a means of increasing the check average. Perhaps the standard script is to describe an appetizer to share on the table, or ask the Guests if they would like to preorder an amazing dessert that just so happens to take twenty minutes to prepare. These are great tactics, are incredibly effective in driving sales, and are not unique to the restaurant industry. Grocery stores, retail outlets, online shopping sites and pretty much anywhere things are sold, there is an opportunity to purchase that one last item before checking out.

By now, consumers are hip to those tactics and it has become a customary way of doing business. Not that this fact makes it any less important to incorporate this strategy into our plan, but to be most effective these days, I find that up-selling the *experience* rather than simply the *product* can have much more of an impact.

One great example I have found recently was when I was working with a chef team in a fine dining restaurant. The team was having difficulty communicating with the front of the house staff and conflicts were arising almost on a daily basis. The front of the house managers were complaining that the kitchen would refuse to accommodate certain Guest requests while the kitchen teams felt they were not getting support from the front to run food or with communication about the flow of dining. The energy in the house grew negative and a clear divide became evident between the front and what I refer to as the heart of the house (more commonly referred to as the back of the house). Both teams had lost sight of the true goal of the team as a whole.

The company's mission statement was geared toward providing amazing experiences, and that was clearly impossible to achieve without close cooperation amongst these key players. For several weeks, we worked on practicing more positive and effective communication skills among the Team Members. But perhaps the thing that made the most difference was something that took the focus off the team and redirected it back to where it should have been all along: The Guest.

While learning to communicate better with each other, one of the managers and the chef came up with a plan to give the Guest a great experience, while providing the service team with a tool to make more money. During an exercise in which the teams were asked to recall an amazing Guest experience they had provided in the past, the chef remembered a special dinner that a couple received while dining there. These Guests won a custom five course dinner with wine pairings at a charity auction.

When they came to claim their prize, the chef prepared a beautiful dinner, the wine manager thoughtfully paired each wine and provided a private educational seminar on the history of the wine, how it matched the food and personally butlered the entire experience. The chef came to the table, gave them a tour of the kitchen and sent them away with a signed copy of the menu along with his business card to be used as a personal connection to any of his five restaurants. These Guests were simply blown away by this level of attention and service. They have since recommended the restaurant to many friends and regularly hold their social and business affairs at his establishments.

My heart warmed when I heard of this, and I asked the team what it would be like to give this type of experience to each and every Guest that dined. Of course, at first, this seemed like an impossible task. How could we possibly spend that much time and energy on each and every Guest and still serve the needs of everyone in the restaurant? A five-course dinner with wine pairings would take a lot of resources, and, realistically, not everyone would want that. True; but what if we offered it as an option?

At that, I saw the lights go on for the team, and they began brainstorming ideas on how they could accomplish this. What they came up with was to provide the five-course menu with wine pairings as an in-house option on certain nights at the chef's discretion. This would allow the team the flexibility to decide on the menu and the best nights to execute. Servers would offer the menu as a special experience, and the wine manager and the chef would both be on hand to deliver all of the amazing steps that the original Guests had received. The menu, of course, commanded a higher price point then the average check, so servers were motivated to sell this experience.

At the end of the day, not only were we able to mend the divide among a quarreling team, we were able to align their efforts with the company's mission and give Guests an experience worth talking about. And they did. Soon, Guests would come in just to request this special menu, and it became evident that this restaurant had raised the bar on many fronts.

Building Brand Ambassadors

Assuming our promotions are arranged to bring in many Guests that may be first-time visitors, we must recognize the real opportunity to begin our relationship with them. I once had a manager, Mike, who took the art of connecting with Guests to a new level. He always seemed to carry a sense of pride in making deep connections, and we would often discuss these moments when working on the floor together. Each night, he would eagerly share the interactions he had with our Guests. He seemed to really feel genuine excitement about the idea of someone truly having a great time.

At this restaurant, we were host to many special occasions, and each year, one of those was the celebration of the birthday of the Marine Corps. For this occasion, several high-ranking officers and their families would join together for a nice dinner and several ceremonial activities to honor the ongoing tradition of this distinguished branch of our armed forces. Mike took special pride in this occasion, despite never having served in the military. He simply loved being of service and was always willing to dive deeply into the experience to ensure all of the Guests were wowed. Here is a letter I received from the organizer of the most recent event:

Dear Greg,

I am writing to you to express my sincere gratitude for the most wonderful experience we had last evening while celebrating the birthday of the Marine Corps. Not only was the food, the decor and the service great as usual, but the specific care that was given to our group by Mike is what really made a mark. Having met him on a prior visit while I was dining with my family, he knew that I loved the wide variety of vodkas that you offer. So when he arranged for a special, personalized vodka tasting for our entire group on this occasion, we were completely surprised! What a nice touch and a great way for him to salute our guests of honor. We were also impressed with how closely he tended to the details in support of the execution of some of our traditions, like the cake cutting ceremony. His attention to detail, personalized service and sincere hospitality did not go unnoticed. Please thank him and the rest of the team for a wonderful evening and we will certainly be seeing you again very soon.

With Warm Regards,

Carol

This letter represents an incredibly powerful experience that was created through a sincere desire to be of service to others. When Mike worked to deliver a heartfelt, sincere, emotional encounter, all of the boxes which define true hospitality were checked. I should note that Carol and her family have sent more business back to this restaurant than we would even know. She is out in the community, acting as an ambassador to the brand, due to the viscerally positive experience she and those close to her receive when dining there.

A central part of our promotional plan should always be our Guests. New or returning, each person who steps into our establishment represents an opportunity to connect with them, make them feel like a part of the family, and give them an experience that is so wonderful they will tell everyone they know to come and try it too.

The best form of promotion that we can give often comes when we seize opportunities, like this one, to turn our Guests into raving fans. A program of attraction is marked by the standards we set for ourselves along with how well and how consistently we can execute. What if every Guest felt so compelled to write this type of letter regarding their experience? How many ambassadors of our brand would be out in the community singing our praises and thereby driving more new business into the fold? This type of promotion is far more valuable than any ad we can place, any special we can run, or any deal we can offer.

When we are committed to being of service and showing true hospitality, we will also recognize that every single interaction with a Guest can itself be a promotional opportunity. In these final few sections, I will outline a few more examples as inspiration for how we can serve every day in a way that can turn a first-time Guest into a raving fan.

Everyday Ways to Turn Guests into Raving Fans #1: Little Something Extra

At one of my favorite haunts in Sonoma County, California, great food is paired with craft beer in an environment often charged with live music. Guests can enjoy a different experience than the heavily wine-centric menus the area, known as wine country, typically has on display. Many of their locations offer outdoor seating in a contemporary yet rustic environment.

In the valleys of Sonoma, warm days give way to cool nights. Although most of the space is well heated, the nip of the evening air can still sneak through. The management here has found a creative and impactful solution to this problem. If the air feels cool, staff will offer blankets to Guests as they dine and enjoy the music. This unexpected touch is that little something extra that people truly appreciate. This type of gesture is not made often, and for that reason, it leaves quite an impression. What a way to make people truly feel at home. This little something extra sends a message that the team cares about Guests and their experience.

A well known Chophouse in Suffolk, Virginia is known as an upscale gathering spot for locals. It is a fine dining establishment, but it has a very warm, neighborhood-like appeal. The well-trained team takes the art of hospitality seriously, and it does not take long before you feel a part of the family. At Riverstone, numerous special occasions are celebrated nightly. The dessert will likely come with a candle to commemorate the experience, but it is the presence of the manager that makes all of the difference. Once a table is seated and has had time to settle in, a manager visits the table with a handwritten card signed by the staff. It may read something like this:

Hello, my name is Ken. I am one of the managers here and I just wanted to come by to welcome you and to wish you a truly happy (birthday or other event). We sincerely appreciate that you have chosen to celebrate with us, and I would like to let you know that if there is anything that I can personally do for you while you are here, or in the future, please do not hesitate to ask. I'm happy to help.

This simple gesture instantly creates a rapport and lets the Guest to know that they will be truly taken care of for the rest of the evening. They also feel that they have a trusted ally, a personal connection for future visits.

It is astounding to me how many restaurants never have a manager go by to check on a table during service. Think about it. When was the last time you dined at any restaurant and had a manager come by to ask how things were going, much less to offer their personal assistance? Again, this almost never happens.

What an opportunity it would be to train our management teams to make this a part of their daily routine. Problems could be solved immediately, relationships could be developed, and the heart of hospitality could be intimately felt. Remember, ambassadors of hospitality get involved and stay engaged. This is a crucial element that simply cannot be taken for granted.

Everyday Ways to Turn Guests into Raving Fans #2: Breaking the Rules

As outlined in Chapter Two, our businesses must certainly have policies and procedures. Policies are most often meant to protect the business. We may, and generally should, have strict policies governing things like sexual or unlawful harassment, time and attendance, and various aspects of the work environment itself. Procedures often outline our systems for doing certain things. There may be procedures for things like submitting payroll, counting inventory, administering staff reviews and a host of other activities that help the business run from day to day. When these procedures are not followed, especially in larger or growing companies, quite a bit of chaos can result. When policies are clearly defined and procedures are adhered to, systems tend to operate more smoothly and soundly.

Beyond the realm of policies and procedures, however, lies a set of rules that often go unwritten. These rules tend to be a bit more abstract, yet over the years they have been adopted as industry standard in many businesses. These unwritten rules are often created to serve the self rather than others. For this reason, these rules must sometimes be broken, and new rules might even be developed to replace them.

Let's say my yogurt shop closes at 8 PM each night. The hours are listed on our website, social media accounts, and the front door. Anyone seeking information on our business hours can readily find it. As the business owner, I have every right to close my doors at 8 PM without recourse.

Now let's say that Jon shows up at 8:05 PM with his daughter Veronica. He's promised her a treat of frozen yogurt for a soccer game well played, but her soccer game ran late. The shop has two people in line; one Team Member is helping them and the other is cleaning up and about to lock the door. The rule says that we close at 8 PM. But clearly, we have the ability to serve one more Guest. What will we do?

I can tell you what eighty percent of businesses will likely do. They will say "sorry, we're closed," leaving a very unhappy pair to think twice about returning. This happened to me and my son recently, and what disappointed me more than being turned away was the realization of how common this is in our industry. The young gentleman who sent us away was friendly and well-intended. He was just ignorant to the problem.

It is quite understandable. Young Team Members do not want to break the rules that are made by their employers. They feel that if they make a wrong decision, they will get in trouble. But not everything is black and white. If the yogurt shop Team Member had been trained to decide whether or not to close the door as if he were the owner of the establishment, he might have made a different decision.

This is where we as leaders must teach our teams to manage the gray areas. The fact is, sometimes, we and our Team Members need to break the rules just enough to set ourselves apart.

I once had a disagreement with a chef I hired regarding a split order. At our restaurant, we served a dish comprised of three fish tacos. A couple had ordered the dish and asked that it be split between them. The chef put up two plates, each with one taco and another one that had been sawed in half.

I asked him why he thought it was okay to cut a taco in half. He answered, "It was a split order." I instructed him to give each plate two tacos. He said, "But then we are just giving food away, and we will be training them that it's okay to do that all the time."

I asked the chef how many times he thought this had happened throughout the week, and he admitted that it was rare. I explained to him that, regardless of the rules he thought were in place to protect our business from food loss, in this case, following them was not worth serving a lackluster dish.

I can tell you that if I received a plate with half a taco, no matter if it were my request to split the dish, I would be less than impressed, and I would not likely return any time soon. It would be far better to give away one free taco to make that Guest really happy. I let my chef know that, moving forward, he would need to break the rule in this case in order to support our mission, which must always take precedence.

One great way to break the rules is to invite kids into the kitchen to make their own desserts. This is something that I have done for years, and it makes a huge impact for both the kids and parents, especially in a fine dining setting. In fine dining, sometimes parents can be a bit apprehensive about having their children with them for fear that they will be looked down upon in some way by either the business or other Guests.

In an effort to make everyone feel like family, I love to bring the kids back and allow them to make a sundae or simple dessert. Parents often come to take pictures and the team gets involved as the little ones play chef. Guests will be delighted to see the kids proudly returning to their table with their new creation.

I was once dining at a quaint little bistro with my wife and two young boys. The general manager came by with some chalk and handed it to the kids. Before I had a chance to inquire, she told them that Santa was arriving the next day by train and she needed them to draw some train tracks through the restaurant so that his elves knew where to go. I could not believe that she just turned two little boys loose in the restaurant to draw all over the floor. It was a small place, and she told my wife and I to enjoy ourselves while she kept an eye on the kids. Now, I do not necessarily recommend this for everyone, but man, did she break some serious rules there—and I'm not going to forget that moment anytime soon!

The restaurant does not take reservations, and it's very difficult to get a seat on any given night. I have a feeling that Luna, the general manager, has something to do with that. I have been back many times, and I never get tired of telling that story.

The Bottom Line

There are so many ideas and proven ways to drive business into our restaurants—far too many to use as examples in this book. The point is that we should always be thinking outside the box and be willing to go to extraordinary lengths to deliver extraordinary experiences. Ordinary is lame, and our Guests know it.

We can use the guiding principles set forth in this chapter to focus on the elements that magnetically attract people to our businesses—making sure our promotions are actually driving covers or sales, while delivering incredible value. This is the first step to creating a program of attraction that utilizes the resources inside and around our establishment to turn Guests into enthusiastic brand ambassadors.

But don't limit yourself to the advice I offer here. Look around. Do some research. Talk to others in the industry about what has worked for them. Ask friends, family and Guests what they have experienced in their travels that created a lasting memory for them. Then, take some of these ideas and make them your own. The more we practice this, the more proficient we become, and ultimately, the more success we experience. After all, isn't this the fun part of what we do? It certainly should and can be.

CHAPTER SIX

A PROGRAM OF RECOVERY

"We learn from failure, not from success." – Bram Stoker

One thing is for sure. Something will go wrong today.

For all the planning, organizing, training and knowledge that we possess in our industry, there is no doubt that some mistake that will be made—perhaps multiple mistakes that will lead to problem for a Team Member or a Guest. A Team Member will misread their schedule and fail to show up for work. A cook will misjudge the temperature of a steak and it will go out undercooked. The timing of our processes will be thrown off in some small way, and that will affect the flow of service, and thus our Guests' experience. A Team Member will give someone incorrect information, which will lead to that person becoming upset. A Guest will find a foreign object in her food, a dirty glass, or an unattended bathroom, which will give her a negative impression of our business.

There is no getting around the fact that these things and more can and will happen at some point during our day. Yet more businesses than not are grossly unprepared to react to these events in a way that will protect the business itself. Even more have never considered seeing these unfortunate happenings as golden opportunities to build business and surpass their competitors in a way that is highly impactful.

There is no getting around the fact that these things and more can and will happen at some point during our day. Yet more businesses than not are grossly unprepared to react to these events in a way that will protect the business itself. Even more have never considered seeing these unfortunate happenings as golden opportunities to build business and surpass their competitors in a way that is highly impactful.

In fact, recovering from our mistakes can be one of the most powerful means of building our business by far. It is also one of the most overlooked and underutilized aspects in any business. By having a well-developed program of recovery in place, we can take advantage of these inevitable issues in a way that few others do.

In my seminars, I often ask the group if they have ever had a poor customer service experience. By show of hands, ninety-nine percent will identify as being able to relate to this. I joke that the other one percent must not have heard the question.

The fact is that all of us, at some point in time, have had an experience that has turned us off from wanting to return to a business. For me, it does not take much to simply never return again, especially when multiple things go wrong. Quite frankly, I have far too many options to choose from, and it is much easier simply never to return than to take a chance on a subpar experience. When I ask those who have raised their hands how many of them have taken the opportunity to complain in that moment, rather than simply deal with it and walk away never to return, less than half of the group will usually identify. Keep in mind that this means most dissatisfied Guests simply walk away, never to return—for those Guests, we never have the chance to win them back.

Of those that have again raised their hands, I then ask how many of them feel that their issue was resolved quickly and efficiently. Surprisingly, or perhaps not so surprisingly, a bit more than half of those will identify. I then ask, of those who have identified, how many of them say that they would return to do business there again. Only a small percentage of those hands will stay raised.

What this shows is that, even if a business is given the opportunity to address an issue and takes steps to resolve it, depending on the severity of the pain that was inflicted, there is no guarantee that the affected person will want to return. The odds in cases where we screw up are heavily stacked against us to begin with.

So what will make the difference? There are surely a million and one ways a Guest could be agitated while visiting our business. Sometimes, they are just having a bad day and projecting their discomfort upon us or the situation. But most often it is because we let down what was a high expectation and did not fulfill our commitment to deliver a quality experience. I am not one of those who believe the Guest is always right. Nonetheless, they are still the Guest. As servant leaders, it is not our job to point out right or wrong, but rather to ensure that the experience we provide does not just meet, but far exceeds the expectation.

Opening the Lines

There is little question as to whether feedback is important in our businesses. The question to ask is whether we have a solid understanding of how that feedback is attained and a reliable system of response. Of all of the organizations I have worked with, very few have mastered this concept.

A program of this kind is one of the easiest to overlook or ignore altogether. It's very easy for all of us to turn a blind eye to problems, especially to negative feedback. When the reviews pour in on social media, when managers have to deal with tough conversations concerning upset Guests, when we have to face issues internally, which are often emotionally charged, it is much easier to ignore and hope that no real damage has been done than to face things head-on.

Quite frankly, it can be painful to log onto Yelp and see what people have to say about our businesses in a given week. To this day, I still get an emotional rise as I wait for the page to load. It's stressful. And if it is stressful for me, I can understand why anyone would have problems dealing with issues such as these when they arise; it's so much easier to sweep them under the rug and pretend everything is fine.

But in these cases, everything is *not* fine. It is never okay to just hope for the best and not take control of the situation. Leaving things to chance in the area of recovery is a slippery slope and will never yield the positive results that we need to ultimately be successful. To get past this, to emerge from the mire of fear and discomfort, we must first open the lines of communication by clearly defining the channels through which feedback is received and responded to.

The Face of Feedback

Feedback comes in many forms, but most of it can be categorized in two ways. The first, direct feedback, is what we usually think of when discussing this topic. Someone may email or send a handwritten letter to the company. In a restaurant that has older clientele, handwritten notes are not uncommon. Sometimes a Guest may place a phone call to discuss their concern personally. This is less common, especially in a day and age where people prefer to vent, and may want to avoid any uncomfortable conversation.

Occasionally, we may receive feedback in the form of an in-person conversation. Yet more often than not, the first kind of feedback comes through some type of social media such as Yelp, Facebook, Trip Advisor, or another online review site. People have grown quite comfortable with expressing their views in this way and feel they are doing others a service by letting everyone know what their experience was like.

The rise of this technology has certainly benefited consumers in many ways, but it can easily be seen by businesses as more of a hindrance. Since it's so easy for someone to share a potentially negative experience with thousands of other people this way, social media has become an amplifier for what was once a more internal issue. Word of mouth has become word of the masses. Nonetheless, all of these forms of receiving positive or negative information from our Guests are very clear and direct, making it easy for us to respond to the information being provided. For this reason, we categorize them all as direct feedback.

Still, there is another form of feedback that is not so obvious. This second type of feedback takes a bit more awareness to recognize. It requires being connected to the pulse of what is going on and being in tune with our Guests at all times. Most often this type of feedback is shared through body language or an off-putting look. Or perhaps we hear two people speaking about their experience. Dare I say eavesdropping? Or maybe a regular Guest has stopped coming in. All of these are more subtle forms of feedback that, if we are to detect them, require us to have a more heightened sense of awareness.

But the real question is, regardless of how it comes to us, what are we to do with this feedback? I find when working with owners and managers that there are several scenarios that will often play out; unfortunately, it is rare to see restaurateurs who are utilizing feedback to its full capacity. It can be difficult enough to acknowledge it at all.

The Ostrich Syndrome

Sadly, when comments or criticisms are presented, even in the most direct way, often they are simply ignored. When I bring up Yelp in conversation with a business owner, the reaction can be quite predictable. I am often met with an eye roll, an uncomfortable shift of the shoulders, or even a response like, "I hate Yelp. I wish it would go away." I again admit that even in my own businesses, whenever I think of logging on to check the reviews, I get a bit of a knot in my stomach.

No one likes to be criticized. Especially those of us who have poured our hearts and souls into our business and careers, only to be told how we should be doing our jobs by someone who has no idea of the toils we go through on a daily basis. Often, our natural reaction is to blame the platform through which the complaints come, or to criticize the people who are criticizing us. It is all too easy to simply ignore the reviews and not deal with the emotional strife. We've got enough on our plates, right?

Some of us have gone so far as to ignore phone calls or messages that have come by email. Like ostriches in folk tales, we have stuck our heads in the sand, pretending that an issue does not matter much rather than dealing with it. Or perhaps we have ignored the subtle signs that suggest to us that a Guest is not quite satisfied with something. Rather than dig a little deeper to see what the problem might be, we move on to the next task and hope for the best.

These examples are far more common than we would like to admit. They may seem small, yet as a whole, they amount to a spreading cancer attacking our businesses. By refusing to engage with our Guests and be open to whatever feedback that comes our way, we are closing ourselves off to one of the biggest opportunities we have—to only turn a negative situation around, but to position ourselves in the marketplace as a place of trust and integrity.

As something of real value to our Guests, these qualities simply do not go unnoticed. People quickly learn who will do the right thing and who will not. For this reason, we must not allow ourselves to become a part of the ninety percent of businesses that do not go far enough to invite Guest feedback and to use it as an opportunity to engage. Depending on how we handle this piece of our business, our reputation in the community will ultimately be swayed: Either we will be known for integrity, or we will be known for caring less. It will not take long for that word to get out, and, whether good or bad, it *will* have an impact on our bottom line.

No More Half Measures

Many of us already recognize the importance of answering reviews and responding to direct or indirect forms of feedback. We understand that simply ignoring issues that come up is a refusal to acknowledge the problem and makes for a poor practice. Perhaps we already respond to social media reviews on a regular basis and answer emails and phone calls as they come in, addressing any issues head-on. When we pick up some subtle cues that tell us there is an issue in our presence, we ask how we can help.

Yet we must recognize that sometimes, the response itself is not enough. Acknowledgment of an issue is a great start, but the degree to which we can use this opportunity to create a raving fan is in fact directly proportional to the quality of that response.

Once I worked with a restaurant owner who proudly presented to me that he responded to every Yelp review that came in. His assistant would check the platform daily and respond to each review in the public forum. Both positive and negative reviews would receive a response that others could readily see on the site.

As I scrolled through the reviews, I noticed that he was correct: Every review was being responded to in a timely manner. The problem that I pointed out to him, however, was that each of these responses was obviously copied and pasted for each review with the exact same verbiage. The responses all read something like this: "Please accept our apology for falling short of your expectations. We will take your feedback to heart and hope that you will give us another try."

Immediately, I pointed out that, while his intentions were coming from the right place, this method was not only ineffective, but it was actually doing more damage than good. Yelp users scroll through multiple reviews when trying to decide whether they want to visit a place or not. When they see responses that are cut and pasted, it will always come across as disingenuous and insincere.

What this tells me, as a potential Guest, is that if I have a problem, I will get a stock response with no genuine concern or resolve. This is not something that will motivate me to want to form a relationship with this business. It was a nice try, but this strategy missed the mark. Our responses to complaints and critique must be personal, heartfelt and offer a real solution. Our responses cannot be this kind of half-measure.

I recommended that my client respond to negative reviews with something more like this:

Dear (first name),

Thank you so much for taking the time to express your concerns. We truly value your feedback and pledge to make good use of it by further training our teams for a better outcome in the future.

Please accept our sincerest apologies for falling short of your expectations. I realize your time is valuable and so as a thank you for reaching out I would love to send to you a certificate in the mail towards your next visit with us, assuming you would see fit to return.

All I would need is your mailing address. If you would like to speak to me directly, please feel free to call my cell phone at 555.555.5555 or email me at me@mywebsite.com. I will be more than happy to be a personal resource for you moving forward, so please do not hesitate to reach out.

With Warm Regards,

Greg

I then suggested that my client respond in this way in the private forum rather than the public. This would allow him the ability to offer a personalized solution without broadcasting that he was giving away certificates to anyone who would complain.

Publicly responding to negative reviews makes it difficult to not seem redundant in our response. Guests can easily see how we have responded to others, and if it seems like a cut-and-paste solution that we are providing, it will surely come off as insincere. It is incredibly important to address the Guest in a personal, heartfelt way, and receiving a private message feels much more personal to those who receive it.

Strangely, even though people have no problem broadcasting their complaints openly, they tend to take kindly to more personal, private resolution. That business owner has since shared with me many stories of Guests who have happily returned to give him another try with a certificate, a measure which, notably, can be tracked to ensure it is providing a return.

Similarly, we will want to avoid using half-measures when given the opportunity to go deeper with a Guest who seems like something is a little off, but who does not want to make a big deal about the situation.

Often, when people are dining at a restaurant, especially with friends or family, they shy away from complaining about something that may be really bothering them out of fear of embarrassment or causing a scene. Sometimes, it is our job to detect when this is happening and to find a way to let these Guests know that we are willing to do whatever it takes to make sure they do not leave disappointed.

By being present in the dining room and tuning in to our Guests' emotions, we are more apt to recognize these situations when they occur. If I am walking by a table and a Guest seems to have a sour look, or if I overhear them complaining quietly to their friends about the quality of the dish or service, I could view this as a nuisance and prepare to deflect and make excuses. Or, I could realize that I now have an opportunity to quickly engage to see if I may be of assistance, turning a negative experience into a positive connection. Once again, addressing the issue is halfway there, but it is the quality of our solution that will make the difference in developing a lasting relationship.

C.A.R.E.S.

I have never been a huge fan of acronyms, but I could not resist using one to illustrate the elements that must be present in any effective program of recovery. In order to turn a negative experience into a meaningful relationship, we must not simply put a Band-Aid on the problem. We must come to the table with a sincere desire, not only to apologize, but to gain a new trusted friend and to become a resource for them moving forward. Our goal should always be to personalize the experience and to make a deep connection.

Where a Guest once felt left out in the cold and unrecognized, we must now make them feel as if they are the most important part of the equation. Where they once felt wronged, we must make things right. And we can do this by making sure we practice several simple but very important principles.

C.A.R.E.S. #1: Connection

The first thing we must do is *connect* with our Guests. Those whom we serve must always have full and complete access to us. This must happen at every stage of communication.

Many quick-service restaurants have a corporate 800 number posted at the drive-through asking for Guests to provide feedback at any time. This provides people a direct line of communication should something go wrong or should they feel the need to express their opinion about a product or their experience.

At one local coffee shop, there is a sign at the counter with a note from the owner that says:

Let us help before you Yelp. We would love your feedback! If there is any issue that we have not been able to successfully solve for you here, call me on my cell phone at 555-555-5555. -(Owner)

This method allows people to connect in a very personal way, and it sends the powerful message that they have a direct line to the owner should anything go wrong. It simply expresses, "we care."

As a general manager, I always had my cell phone number listed on my business card. This would allow me to let people know that, should they need me for any reason, I would be very easy to reach and could act as a personal resource for them. Some thought I was crazy for printing my personal phone number and giving it out to thousands of people, but very few ever actually used it. Having that number available to people easily gives them direct access to me; it feels good to Guests to know they have a direct line to the boss.

Connections also happen by making ourselves personally available. In my restaurants, managers are expected to visit each and every table, every single shift. Their goal is to personally check on each Guest's experience and to make a connection early on, so that, should a problem arise, the Guest already knows that they have an ally close by.

When I ask people the last time they remember going to any restaurant in which the manager visited the table to introduce themselves and to welcome them, I always get similar responses. Most cannot remember a time like this at all. Some remember a visit when something went wrong; almost no one can remember a manager visiting purely as a means to connect and invite friendship. With this type of interaction being so rare in most establishments, adopting and implementing a culture of this kind of connection with Guests gives us a huge competitive advantage.

In addition to always keeping management on the front lines, close to those they serve, my teams are always trained to let the manager know at even the slightest hint of something being wrong. With my teams, my direction will always be: "If the ice is too cold, we want to know about it." This gives us another line of connection directly to our Guests, even when we are not physically present. If everyone is trained to sound the alarm when something is even remotely wrong, we will always have the opportunity to react quickly and turn that problem into an opportunity to serve.

C.A.R.E.S. #2: Accountability

I have never been a fan of the phrase "the customer is always right." In fact, they are not always right. *No one* is always right. As I briefly referenced earlier in this chapter, I prefer to align with the idea that yes, the Guest is not always right—but they are always the Guest.

The idea that in every situation someone is right and someone is wrong can be a very slippery slope. The last thing that we should be doing when addressing an issue is to assign right and wrong to the situation. When this happens, we may be tempted to make excuses for the situation, or worse, to "educate" the Guest.

Let's say that one of our Guests has ordered a steak to be cooked medium rare. When the server goes to check on the table to see how everything is, this Guest comments that the steak is overcooked and that he would like a new one. When the server returns the steak to the kitchen, the chef inspects the steak and it is, in fact, a perfect medium rare. At this point, we have a choice. We can return to the table to let know that the steak was, in fact, cooked properly. Or, we can accept the fact that the Guest is technically wrong in this situation, and prepare a steak more to what his vision for medium rare is.

Which of these two scenarios do we think will get a better response? Which of these is in line with our mission? The fact is, no amount of trying to educate this Guest on how a steak should be prepared is going to improve his experience.

And we must ultimately take one hundred percent responsibility for the Guest's experience. Anything short of this will result in certain disaster. The trust that we have built up to that point will quickly erode, and our Guest will be lost. In this situation, we may ask probing questions to ensure that we can cook the steak to an idea of medium rare that matches what the Guest wants, but we never want to come off as argumentative or condescending. This is a very delicate dance, and it requires a great deal of empathy and a strong desire to please.

Early in my marriage I learned a very valuable lesson regarding taking full responsibility in any relationship. My wife and I had been quarreling over a sponge for weeks. I found nothing wrong with placing the sponge on the center divider between the two sinks in our kitchen. Every day, she would make it known that she did not want this sponge to rest there; rather, it should be placed in the sponge holder she had specifically purchased.

For the life of me, I could not understand why this was such a big deal. My thoughts went something like this: *I mean, it's a freaking sponge, and it belongs at the sink. Who cares where it rests?* My wife had even gone to the length of stretching some masking tape along the sink divider and writing the word "sponge" in a circle with a line through it. When I sat the sponge on top of her sign, the roof came down and we had it out. In a dramatic shouting match, I asked, "What's the big ******* deal?"

To which she replied, with tears (and a wild look) in her eyes, "It's not about the sponge, you ***... It's because it's IMPORTANT TO ME!"

I am not sure exactly how many seconds it took for me to feel deflated, but at that moment, I learned one of the most important lessons of my entire relationship with her. In fact, this lesson has changed the quality of every relationship in my life from that day forward. Later that day, I replaced my wife's masking tape sign with one of my own. It read, "It's important to her." I never (well almost never) put that sponge there again; and I do my best to live by the principal that if something is important to my wife, then, by default, it simply MUST become important to me.

As deeply as this rings true for a relationship as intimate as a marriage, it also applies to *any* relationship for which we have a responsibility to serve. Serving our Guests in our restaurants should be every bit as intimate with regard to this principle. We must simply care that much. When we do, our Guests and Team Members will feel it. And they will respond in kind by investing their time and energy—and money—back into our business again and again.

C.A.R.E.S. #3: Responsiveness

When an emergency occurs, such as a robbery or a fire, the response time of the team that is called to assist is critical. If we are dealing with a life-or-death situation, how quickly the police or fire department is able to respond to the situation can mean the difference between a positive outcome or something much more devastating. In the restaurant industry, we are not likely to be dealing with these types of life-or-death situations, but in many cases, the meaning that's placed upon the experience of those who visit our business is no less important.

In fine dining, most people are celebrating a special occasion, dining with someone they care for, or perhaps with someone they would like to impress. For these people, the stakes are high. They are investing a good deal of money in the hopes for an amazing experience that will produce a heightened emotional outcome.

In casual dining, there may be less of an expectation in terms of the overall experience, but when something goes wrong, a speedy solution to the problem is no less important. When we visit a business and a mistake is made, most of us can easily forgive, especially when we can see it was a simple error. But when we have an issue that needs to be addressed, some problem that only someone within the company can solve for us, the longer it takes to make that connection, the faster we lose faith in the relationship overall, and the more likely we will choose a competitor on our next outing.

Responding quickly to problems lets people know that we are in tune with the needs of those we serve and that we are willing to do what it takes to make sure they feel supported. From the Guest's perspective, the time it takes us to respond to any problem is directly proportional to the degree to which we care. The longer the response time, the less we are perceived as caring.

For this reason, we must always be alert and ready to respond to any issue. This means monitoring our social media daily. It means responding to emails and phone messages the same day, ideally within a few short hours. It means heading into the fire immediately as we are made aware of issues on-site. I share with my teams that when issues arise, we are like first responders. We must not wait until the flames engulf the building. Instead, we must head directly to the problem in an effort to snuff out any spark that could turn into a blaze.

Remember that waiting equals wondering. If a Guest has made us aware of an issue that they are having and need us to help solve it, allowing them to wait also allows them to wonder. They will wonder first if their message was received. They will wonder if anyone is listening to their concern. They will wonder if we even care. And if no response is received, they will likely conclude that we simply do not and will not care about them moving forward. At that point, we have lost them, perhaps forever.

C.A.R.E.S. #4: Empathy

In dealing with any issue that arises, we must show a sincere and genuine concern for the Guest's perspective. Remember: It is important to them. Therefore, it must now be important to us. By putting ourselves in their shoes, we can better empathize with the situation they are experiencing.

Whenever I am dealing with a complaint, if possible, I will sit down with the Guest so I am physically on their level. This creates an air of partnership and allows us to connect. We will want to look our partner in the eye with a soft gaze and listen deeply.

I stress deeply because it is all too easy to pretend that we are hearing someone while simply readying to fire back with an explanation or an excuse. When emotions are high, it is incredibly important that we own our part and hold the space for our Guests to vent their frustrations. Most people simply want to be heard and acknowledged in these situations, and the more effectively we are able to allow this, the more successful we will be in the recovery process.

We must apologize sincerely and wholeheartedly for the problem. It does not matter at this point if anyone is right or wrong in the situation. It only requires us taking one hundred percent responsibility for what our partner in this discussion—our Guest—is feeling. We must never make excuses or educate our partner. We must simply apologize and vow to make it right.

It is always helpful to thank them for caring enough to reach out to let us know about this problem. We must always do our best to make the Guest the superstar in this equation. If we see her as someone who is just complaining and making our life difficult, we will naturally project that energy back to her. But if we praise this person and acknowledge the fact that she has taken time out of her very busy day to make us aware of the issue, and that we are incredibly grateful for that effort, we will be positioning ourselves in such a way that this Guest can only walk away feeling good about the outcome. Even if they were reaching out in anger, we will always want to thank them for reaching out. This will defuse the situation and allow for the possibility of a resolution.

C.A.R.E.S. #5: Solution

Besides simply being heard, what people want most when they complain about a problem is for something to be done about it. They want a solution.

In my experience, this is where many businesses fall short. It must always be our goal to provide a powerful solution that will not only fix the problem, but motivate someone to return and to recommend our business to others.

There is a strong emphasis here on the word powerful. Ordinary solutions, just like ordinary expectations, fall far short of our goal. People expect ordinary. They expect that we will do just enough to say that we are sorry, but nothing more. In order to be truly effective, we must personalize the experience and be willing and ready to go above and beyond that expectation.

Remember that at this point, we have lost the trust in the relationship. We must now begin to rebuild that trust if we are to make our troubled Guest a raving fan.

When someone has written a negative review on social media, my teams are trained to respond quickly with a personal, heartfelt apology and to offer their direct contact information so that a personal connection can be made. I will always give the reviewer my cell phone number as a means to connect so that we can have a personal conversation about a solution. If this person is willing to connect in this way, we will always reach a positive resolve.

If a complaint was made by letter, phone message, or email, my teams will always personally respond in the same manner, doing their best connect with the Guest so that we can fully understand the nature of their complaint and deliver a very timely, personal, and thorough solution.

An example of an email response might be:

Dear Jane,

I recently received your email regarding your experience with us last Saturday. First, I would like to express my sincerest and deepest apology for the shortcomings that you experienced. We pride ourselves on delivering amazing experiences and for the fact that we fell short on this occasion pains me deeply. Please know that we will be taking all of your feedback to heart and using it as a training tool for our team moving forward.

Next, as a thank you for reaching out to us, I would love the opportunity to send you a certificate in the mail toward your next visit, assuming you would see fit to return. All I would need is your mailing address.

Lastly, should there be anything that I can personally do for you moving forward at this or any of our restaurants, please do not hesitate to reach out to me directly at my contact information listed below. I would like to remain a personal resource for you with us as well as our network of partners, so please do not be shy to reach out.

If given the opportunity, we sincerely look forward to welcoming you back with open arms so please let us know how we may help.

With Warm Regards,

Greg

The same type of verbiage would likely be used when speaking to a Guest directly or over the phone. If the situation is more dire, we may want to personally invite the Guest back for a complete new experience with our compliments to show them what we are truly capable of. Regardless of the solution itself, if we are connecting with the Guest, offering a solution that is above and beyond, and positioning ourselves as a personal resource moving forward, there is almost no one who can resist allowing the opportunity for us to rebuild the relationship. In fact, if we are known to address issues in this way, many of these Guests will become our most loyal fans moving forward.

The Bottom Line

An effective program of recovery can be one of the greatest opportunities we have to create return business. Yet it is by far the most poorly executed and overlooked aspect in business today. Still, if we follow the principles set forth in C.A.R.E.S., taking accountability, focusing on our Guests' feelings, and providing a solution that goes above and beyond, out of these painful experiences, some of our most lasting relationships can be born. When treated with empathy, sincerity, and a heartfelt desire to deliver true hospitality, our Guests will respond in kind, and continue to invest their time, energy, money, and life events with us for years to come.

FINAL THOUGHTS

"Alone we can do so little; together we can do so much." – Helen Keller

---

Everything about this book has been a collaborative effort. The stories and examples are all based on real people and actual businesses. Each and every one of those experiences brought with it a lesson. That is the entire reason I wrote this book to begin with. I have been incredibly fortunate to have partnered with so many amazing people and organizations throughout my career, and the experiences I have had with each of these opportunities have shaped not only my own businesses but those whom I've had the pleasure to serve.

For some of you, this book may be just the beginning of an amazing journey full of success, failure and everything in between. For others, it may have served as a reminder to get back to the basics. Still others may be wondering how to put some of these ideas further into practice for themselves. Regardless of your path, if you take away nothing more from this book than a greater motivation to improve your own experience, the experience of your Guests and those whom you employ, then we can all consider that a win!

If, at any time, you feel the need to explore these principles further and need a partner with whom to do so—or if you simply have questions about the concepts within or how to apply them to your specific business—do not hesitate to contact me directly at my contact information, listed at the end of this chapter. My mission is to serve you and to give what I have found in an attempt to better your business, and perhaps your life.

And feel free to share this book with others! The more of us who learn to grow our businesses organically and with heart, the better we can make the world. Sound like a pie-in-the-sky type of proposition? I invite you to try it on. Employing the principles in this book with even a fair degree of consistency will surely reap almost immediate benefits. Once you decide to join the top five percent of us who truly understand the power of employing the X-Factor, living our mission, attracting Guests through experienced-based promotions, and mastering the art of recovery, you will certainly begin the find greater joy, fulfillment and profits over the long term.

I wish for you more success, more joy, and more profitability than you can possibly enjoy in this lifetime.

Yours In Service,

Greg Provance

GPHospitalityPartners.com

greg@GPHospitalityPartners.com

ACKNOWLEDGEMENTS

Without the help and mentorship of the following people, and many more that are not specifically named here, this book would not have been possible. A special thank you goes out to:

Carre Provance, my incredible wife and life partner. Without your love and support, nothing is possible.

David and Lesley Cohn, for creating and growing a model of business that shaped my philosophy of leadership.

Chef Deborah Scott, for your friendship and partnership over the years.

Chef Gerry Garvin, whose example inspired me to see the restaurant industry as not only a career, but a way of life.

Trevor Watkins, for your unwavering friendship and for supporting all of my crazy ideas.

Maurice Denis, coach, mentor and friend.

Ken Dodd, for laying the path as a leader and restauranteur.

Brett Meltzer, for your endless energy and enthusiasm.

John Abate, spiritual guru, whose guidance got me over the hump and continues to inspire and inform.

Drew Davis, strategic partner and trail-running mate.

John Sarkisian, for your giant entrepreneurial spirit, partnership and friendship.

Michael Pirraglia, friend, colleague and partner in business and life.

Phoenix Bunke, editor extraordinaire and really cool gal.

And many, many others whom I have had the pleasure and good fortune to have encountered and worked alongside over the years. The spirit of those experiences are represented here.